Definitions

Though trafficking in women is a longstanding issue globally, it is a relatively new issue for US policymakers. US policymakers are struggling to better understand the phenomenon, with some officials viewing it as an alien smuggling issue and others viewing it through a human rights prism. Trafficking in humans may share common characteristics with alien smuggling and illegal immigration, but it has its own distinctive features and dynamics involving particularly grievous human rights abuses.

As a first step, it is important to be clear on the definition of trafficking in women, as the characterization of the issue will determine the strategies to combat the problem and protect the victims. The President's Interagency Council on Women, chaired by the Secretary of State, leads the coordination of US domestic and international policy on the trafficking in women issue. The President's Interagency Council on Women has formulated a definition on trafficking in women and children:

- ***Trafficking*** *is all acts involved in the recruitment, abduction, transport, harboring, transfer, sale or receipt of persons; within national or across international borders; through force, coercion, fraud or deception; to place persons in situations of slavery or slavery-like conditions, forced labor or services, such as forced prostitution or sexual services, domestic servitude, bonded sweatshop labor or other debt bondage.* [3]

In essence, trafficking in women is the use of force and deception to transfer women into situations of extreme exploitation. Examples of this may include Latvian women threatened and forced to dance nude in Chicago; Thai women brought to the US for the sex industry, but then forced to be virtual sex slaves; ethnically Korean-Chinese women held as indentured servants in the Commonwealth of the Northern Mariana Islands; and hearing-impaired and mute Mexicans brought to the US, enslaved, beaten, and forced to peddle trinkets in New York City.[4]

---

[3] It should be noted that trafficking is also defined in the "International Protocol to Prevent, Suppress, and Punish Trafficking in Persons, especially Women and Children," which will be a supplement to the UN Convention Against Transnational Organized Crime. This Protocol and Convention are currently under negotiation.

According to the Protocol, trafficking in persons means the recruitment, transportation, transfer, harboring or receipt of persons: by the threat or use of kidnapping, force, fraud, deception or coercion, or by the giving or receiving of unlawful payments or benefits to achieve the consent of a person having control over another person, for the purpose of sexual exploitation* or forced labor.

The word "sexual exploitation" is being debated, and may be replaced by the words servitude and slavery.

Given the wide range of trafficking cases that occur in the US, debates on the definition often focus on whether or not the women were witting or unwitting about the type of work. It makes no legal difference, however, whether or not the victim initially knew or agreed to perform the labor voluntarily. A person cannot consent to enslavement or forced labor of any kind. The Thirteenth Amendment outlawing slavery prohibits an individual from selling himself or herself into bondage, and Western legal tradition prohibits contracts consenting in advance to assaults and other criminal wrongs. If a person desires to stop performing the work, and then is forced to remain and perform the job against his or her will, then the work is involuntary regardless of the victim's purported consent.[5]

The use of force—be it physical or psychological—to hold someone against his or her will has also been debated when discussing the definition. Some defense attorneys for the traffickers have sought to argue that if there was no physical confinement of the victims, there was no captivity. US law, nonetheless, recognizes that more subtle forms of restraint can be used to detain someone, and the victims' vulnerabilities are relevant. If defendants use force, threats of force, or threats of legal coercion to create a "climate of fear" to compel service, they are guilty of involuntary servitude.[6] Additionally, the definition of force or coercion in the draft version of the International Protocol to Prevent, Suppress, and Punish Trafficking in Persons especially Women and Children encompasses both physical and psychological coercion.

- **Force or coercion** *includes obtaining or maintaining through act or threat the labor, services, or other activities of a person by physical, legal, psychological or mental coercion, or abuse of authority. Force or coercion also entails a person's reasonable belief that he has no viable alternative but to perform the work, service or activity, whether that is objectively correct or not. The definition also includes an extortionate extension of credit and debt bondage; threats of force, harm or violence to the victim or the victim's family; or unlawful restriction of movement and liberty, though this is not a necessary element.*

In addition to force and coercion, another subject of frequent discussion is the degree of organized crime involvement in the trafficking industry in the US, and the definition of organized crime. Traditionally, organized crime is associated with self-perpetuating, hierarchical criminal organizations, such as the infamous Italian mafia families.[7] The definition of organized crime used by the UN Convention

---

[4] Men were also trafficked in this case, and to the Northern Mariana Islands to be indentured servants.

[5] Department of Justice Manual for Prosecuting Worker Exploitation Cases.

[6] Department of Justice Manual for Prosecuting Worker Exploitation Cases.

against Transnational Organized Crime—which is under current negotiation and scheduled to ready for ratification by the end of 2000—identifies smaller, less organized structures.

• An **organized criminal group** *is a structured group of three or more persons existing for a period of time and having the aim of committing a serious crime in order to, directly or indirectly, obtain a financial or other material benefit.*

This definition encompasses a broader spectrum of crime affiliation encompassing smaller crime groups, loosely connected criminal networks, or large organized families, and more appropriately describes organized crime involvement in trafficking in the US.

In reviewing the major trafficking cases in the United States since 1990, the perpetrators tended to be smaller crime groups, smuggling rings, gangs, loosely linked criminal networks, and corrupt individuals who tended to victimize their own nationals. None of the traffickers' names were found in the International Criminal Police Organization's database indicating that these traffickers were not under investigation for trafficking or other illicit activities in other countries. This contrasts with Europe and Asia where there are more indications of large, hierarchical structures involved in trafficking women and children and numerous other illegal activities.

The size or structure of the criminal group, however, has no bearing on the violence, intimidation, and brutality that is commonly perpetrated on the trafficking victims, as many small trafficking rings are extremely vicious. Moreover, technology has made size irrelevant in terms of a crime group's ability to establish commercial or business-like structures. The traffickers have easily established businesses in the US and abroad to conceal their activities and illicit proceeds from law enforcement as well as to deceive the women.

It is also important to recognize that only tentative conclusions regarding the level of organized crime involvement in the trafficking industry in the US can be reached at this point as the subject has received little attention from law enforcement. US law enforcement officers readily admit they do not know to what degree large international organized crime syndicates are engaged in this industry. Asian and

---

[7] Organized crime is generally defined by US law enforcement agencies as criminal acts committed by self-perpetuating, structured, and disciplined associations of individuals or groups combined together in a hierarchical or coordinated manner. Their activities are generally conspiratorial and tend to insulate their leadership from direct involvement. Their primary goal is economic gain from illegal activities.

Russian organized crime groups are clearly present in the US and involved in alien smuggling and/or prostitution among other illicit activities. Some experts state that these large criminal syndicates are also involved in trafficking in women, and they will become even more immersed in trafficking to the US given the industry's extensive profits. In order to reach more definitive findings about the present and future role of organized crime in the trafficking industry, more resources need to be devoted towards bolstering research and data collection.

Table of Contents

I. Trafficking: The Global Nexus

Trafficking in persons, especially women and children, this modern-day form of slavery, is prevalent across the globe and likely to increase in the United States. In this post-Cold War era, international borders and political entities mean less while economic issues mean more. Today, threats to society—such as international organized crime, terrorism, weapons of mass destruction and cyber attacks on our critical communications infrastructure—are both unconventional and destabilizing. As Attorney General Reno has said repeatedly, "all crime is international in its consequences." Traffickers in woman and children, much like terrorists and narcotics traffickers, operate boldly across sovereign borders. They have not only capitalized on technological and communications advancements, which have facilitated the flow of goods and people, but have also exploited the economic crises in Russia and Asia as well as regional conflicts, such as Kosovo.

Traffickers have taken advantage of the unequal status of women and girls in the source and transit countries, including harmful stereotypes of women as property, commodities, servants, and sexual objects. Traffickers have also taken advantage of the demand for cheap, unprotected labor, and the promotion of sex tourism in some countries.[1] To the traffickers, people are highly profitable, low risk, expendable, reusable, and resellable commodities. Whereas alien smuggling usually involves short-term monetary profit, trafficking usually involves long-term exploitation for economic gain. Organized crime groups profit from both the trafficking fees and the trafficked person's labor. In some cases, the traffickers may profit even further by using the trafficked persons as "manpower" for other criminal purposes, such as selling drugs.[2]

The trafficking industry worldwide also is closely intertwined with other related criminal activities, such as extortion, racketeering, money laundering, bribery of public officials, drug use, and gambling. For example, INS raids on brothels run by traffickers in Toronto have netted heroin and counterfeit currency. And the Wah Ching, an Asian organized crime group engaged in smuggling and trafficking Asian women, is also involved in gambling, robbery, murder, drug trafficking, and loan sharking. The Wah Ching also has connections to Asian organized crime groups in Boston, New York City, Los Angeles, Seattle, Dallas, Vancouver, and Toronto.[3] Trafficking also usually involves conspiracy, document forgery, visa, mail, and wire fraud. Even in the United States, some traffickers have been known to supply the women with fraudulent state identification and social security cards. This involvement in a multitude of criminal activities and ties among various criminal associations only serves to increase the burden on local and federal law enforcement agencies.

Trafficking into the sex industry also has serious societal consequences as it contributes to the spread of HIV and AIDS. Some trafficked women are required to engage in unprotected sex. Particularly disturbing is a case uncovered by INS where at least one trafficker was purchasing HIV-positive females because he found them to be cheap labor and since he believed they had nothing to live for.

Moreover, the corruption commonly associated with the trafficking industry in many source, transit, and destination countries serves to undermine law enforcement and the rule of law. Many non-governmental organizations stress that the trafficking

---

[1] Miller, Ali and Stewart, Alison, Report from the Roundtable on The Meaning of Trafficking in Persons: A Human Rights Perspective, Women's Rights Law Reporter, Rutgers Law School, Fall/Winter 1998. Vol. 20 Number 1.

[2] International Center for Migration Policy Development, "Draft Study on the Relationship Between Organised Crime and Trafficking in Aliens," Prepared by the Secretariat of the Budapest Group, Vienna, Austria January 1999.
[3] Operation Lost Thai, Special Report, September 1999.

industry could not exist and thrive without corruption. The ripple effects of trafficking are enormous, as it is a political, economic, crime, health, migration, and most importantly, a human rights issue.

Overall, the global nexus of trafficking has fundamental policy implications. Isolated country efforts to combat trafficking will mean little without a larger coordinated international effort. The transnational character of trafficking means that the countries of origin, transit, and destination must work together collaboratively.

II. Scope and Magnitude

Trafficking in persons, particularly women and children, is significant on nearly every continent. Gauging the level of trafficking with precision, however, is difficult since it is an underground industry. Estimates of the trafficking problem in the United States vary, given differing definitions of what constitutes trafficking and research based on limited case studies. At present, no one US or international agency is compiling accurate statistics. Nonetheless, government and non-governmental experts in the field estimate that out of the 700,000 to two million[4] women and children who are trafficked globally each year, 45,000 to 50,000 of those women and children are trafficked to the United States. Approximately 30,000 women and children are being trafficked annually from Southeast Asia, 10,000 from Latin America, 4,000 from the Newly Independent States and Eastern Europe, and 1,000 from other regions.[5]

There have been reports of trafficking instances in at least 20 different states, with most cases occurring in New York, California, and Florida. Some Florida law enforcement officials, for example, claim that the state is being inundated with trafficked women from Russia, Ukraine, and Central Europe. INS and Labor Department officials fear that the problem is not only bigger than they thought but also getting worse. For example, INS has discovered over 250 brothels in 26 different cities,[6] which likely involved trafficking victims. Evidence suggests that state and local law enforcement officials appear to have only scratched the surface of the problem. Trafficking cases are hard to uncover as the crime usually occurs "behind closed doors," and language and cultural barriers usually isolate the victims.

The primary source countries for the United States appear to be Thailand, Vietnam, China, Mexico, Russia, Ukraine, and the Czech Republic. Women have also been trafficked to the US from the Philippines, Korea, Malaysia, Latvia, Hungary, Poland, Brazil, and Honduras among other countries. Women have been trafficked to the US primarily for the sex industry (prostitution, stripping, peep and touch shows, and massage parlors that offer a variety of sexual services), sweatshop labor, domestic servitude, and agricultural work. Women have also been trafficked to provide maid services at motels and hotels, peddle trinkets on subways and buses, and beg. The average age of the trafficking victim in the United States is roughly 20 years old. Some of the Asian women may have been initially trafficked overseas at a much younger age, but then worked in cities such as Bangkok before being trafficked to the US.[7]

A review of several illustrative trafficking and slavery operations—involving sweatshop, agricultural, and other forms of labor—over the last eight years shows that these operations went unnoticed or were able to exist longer than trafficking operations involving the sex industry. Labor trafficking operations generally lasted from 4½ to 6½ years whereas trafficking operations for prostitution lasted from a little over a year to approximately 2½ years before being discovered. Trafficking operations for other forms of the sex industry, such as exotic dancing and peep-and-touch shows, were in existence for anywhere from 10 months to 3 years. Once uncovered, trafficking and slavery cases usually take about a year and a half to investigate and prosecute, according to the Department of Justice's Involuntary Servitude Coordinator in the Civil Rights Division, Criminal Section.

---

[4] This number is only a preliminary estimate and represents cross-border and international trafficking. It does not include internal trafficking within countries such as Thailand or India.
[5] Central Intelligence Agency briefing, Global Trafficking in Women and Children: Assessing the Magnitude, April 1999.
[6] Operation Lost Thai report.

---

[7] Interview with the Department of Justice's Civil Rights Division, Criminal Section, April 1999.

Intentionally Left Blank

III. Enticement and Deception

Traffickers typically lure women to the United States with false promises of jobs as waitresses, nannies, models, factory workers, or exotic dancers. Capitalizing on rising unemployment, disintegrating social networks, and the low status of women in the source countries, the traffickers promise high wages and good working conditions in exciting US cities. Traffickers recruit women abroad through advertisements and employment, travel, model, or matchmaking agencies. Many women fall victim when they apply for work at seemingly reputable employment agencies which are unlicensed or unregulated. Recruiters may also target beauty contest winners and entice them with "work offers." Additionally, traffickers send recruiters to villages and towns. In other instances, friends and acquaintances recruit women informally, through word of mouth. In almost all the cases, recruiters or agents front the money for provision of travel documents, transportation, and supposed jobs. Occasionally, bogus contracts are used to provide an image of legitimacy, lulling the woman into believing she is dealing with a reputable business.[8] The Coalition Against Trafficking in Women (CATW) reports that the Internet is the latest place for promoting global trafficking of women and children as it is being used to lure women to foreign cities with false promises.[9]

Once recruited, the women usually find themselves in situations with severely curtailed freedoms. The women's passports or travel documents are taken, their movements are restricted, and their wages are withheld until their smuggling debt is repaid. And because traffickers can also re-sell the women's debts to other traffickers or employers, victims are often caught in a cycle of perpetual debt bondage.[10] Women are prevented from leaving by security guards, violence, threats, debt bondage, and/or retention of their documents. The traffickers may maintain control through isolation; in many cases, the women must live and work at the location. The women may also be denied outside medical assistance when needed. Threats of physical abuse against themselves and/or their families are also common in order to force cooperation. Traffickers also play upon the women's fears of arrest and deportation. In additional cases, trafficking victims suffer extreme physical and mental abuse, including rape, imprisonment, forced abortions, and physical brutality.

---

[8] Global Survival Network, "Crime and Servitude: An Expose of the Traffic in Women for Prostitution from the Newly Independent States," October 1997.

[9] Hughes, Donna, Coalition Against Trafficking in Women, Pimps and Predators on the Internet, Globalizing the Sexual Exploitation of Women and Children, March 1999.
[10] USAID Office of Women in Development, Gender Matters Quarterly, "Women as Chattel: The Emerging Global Market in Trafficking," February 1999.

Intentionally Left Blank

IV. Entry Into the US

Women are primarily brought into the US in the following three ways: the illegal use of "legitimate" travel documents, impostor passports, and entry without inspection.

The Illegal Use of Legitimate Travel Documents.

The easiest way to traffic women into the US is for the women to overstay their visa. Traffickers in the Newly Independent States (NIS), Central and Eastern Europe, and Asia commonly use business (B1) and tourist (B2) visas to bring women into the US[11] The visa's time length varies from country to country.[12] This time length is important given that fraud patterns show many passports are recycled for new recruits, thus the longer the visa time length, the greater the room for abuse. In Russia and Ukraine, for example, it is possible to get a multiple entry visa for up to three months whereas in Latvia, the Czech Republic, and Poland it is possible to get a multiple entry visa for up to ten years. Ten-year multiple entry visas are also possible to get in other major source countries, such as Mexico, Thailand, the Philippines, and the PRC.[13]

Student (F1), fiancée (K1), and entertainer visas (P1, P3) are also used to acquire entry. Traffickers have previously illegally purchased I-20 student forms to facilitate obtaining student visas. One trafficker paid a collaborator, with connections within the Los Angeles university system, $6,000 to secure a student visa for an applicant.[14]

Regardless of the type of visa, traffickers often coach the women on how to respond in their visa interview.[15] Fraudulent job letters, employment records, or bank statements are also being used as supporting documentation to obtain the visas and convince a consulate officer that the woman will return.[16] In other trafficking situations, the woman hands over her passport, believing the travel agency or recruiter is handling all of the logistics, including obtaining legitimate work permits. This increases the control that the recruiter has over the women.

One area that traffickers have abused is the travel agency referral program. The program is intended to assist some overburdened embassies in expediting the visa process by allowing travel agencies to refer visa applicants; however, these same overworked embassies often do not have the time and resources to investigate all of the travel agencies in the program. Traffickers have used travel agencies as fronts in order to submit visa applications through the travel agency referral program.[17] In some cases, the travel agency is used unwittingly by the traffickers. As many travel agencies in Asia face bankruptcy, they are increasingly tempted to cut corners and fail to verify all of the applicant's employment information. Conversely, in other instances the travel agencies are expanding their services by getting into the lucrative business of manufacturing fake supporting documents.[18]

- This technique was used in 1995 when Thai traffickers and a German national, Ludwig Janak, trafficked Asian women from Thailand to the US Janak used his company, Bavarian Thai International Manpower Company, to

[11] Interview with Diplomatic Security, September 1998.
[12] The time length of the visa is usually based on reciprocity with a foreign country. The US matches whatever type of visa and time length that is granted to American citizens who wish to travel under similar circumstance to that country.
[13] Interview with the State Department's Visa Office, August 1999.
[14] Investigative statements resulting from Operation Lost Thai.

[15] Interview with INS, New York, December 1998; Interview with the Consular Section, American Embassy in Thailand, February 1999.
[16] Interview with the Consular Section, American Embassy in Thailand, February 1999.
[17] Interview with the Department of State's Bureau of Consular Affairs, Office of Fraud Prevention Programs
[18] Cable from the American Embassy in Seoul, 03878, July 1998.

sponsor and submit the visa applications. The applications were generally dropped off in a consular in-box and the embassy would adjudicate the visa requests. Only one woman ever saw a consular officer, and none had ever met Janak as the Thai traffickers arranged all the details.[19]

- Another example of this abuse occurred recently when the American Embassy in Seoul uncovered a trafficking ring which had used the travel agency referral program to obtain visas for at least 91 fraudulent applicants, most of whom were unemployed, young, single, and female. Fake employment documents were submitted from 20 different companies.[20] In a further trafficking case last year, a random consular check uncovered that Hana Tours, a travel agency in Seoul, had been preparing visa applications with bogus employment information to obtain visas for Korean women.[21]

Additionally, traffickers are using other ruses, such as including a number of mala fides travelers in otherwise legitimate tour groups. Alternatively, traffickers may try to flush the system by dropping off 20 to 30 applications, hoping to get five or six women through.[22]

Corruption also facilitates the illegal use of legitimate travel documents. A Czech crime ring, for example, acquired B1/B2 visas by paying off a Czech foreign service national working in the consular section of the US embassy in Prague. The ring also coached the women on what to put into their visa application.[23] Corrupt government authorities may also turn a blind eye to trafficking for a fee. In Russia, the press reports that local authorities are aware of hundreds of phony agencies yet none have been prosecuted. In Thailand, one trafficker claims that another trafficker paid police approximately $12,000 to "turn a blind eye" when the trafficker was found with some 300 passports. Local Thai police have also been known to extort money from potential US visa applicants who are found with counterfeit or photo-altered Thai passports.[24]

Impostor Passports

Asian traffickers commonly use photo substitutions and impostor passports to transport women into the US. Traffickers typically recycle valid passports with genuine visas and alter them with the recruit's picture or try to pass off the recruit as the person in the passport.[25] In some cases, Asian traffickers also use a "jockey," a person who escorts a woman from Asia to the US.[26] This person is typically of Anglo background and will pretend to be the woman's boyfriend, cousin, or husband.[27] At times, he may go so far as to marry the woman on paper. He is there to answer any questions from immigration officials at the ports of entry. Moreover, Asian traffickers try to target ports of entry where they believe immigration or border officials will not be as familiar with Asians. Traffickers may also use late night flights or holidays when fewer officials are on duty.[28]

[19] Interview with INS, New York, December 1998 and May 1999.
[20] Cable from the American Embassy in Seoul, 005569, October 1999.
[21] Cable from the American Embassy in Seoul, 03567, July 1998.
[22] Interview with FBI, New York, December 1998.
[23] Interview with Diplomatic Security, September 1998.

[24] Investigative statements resulting from Operation Lost Thai.
[25] Interview with the Department of State, Consular Affairs, Office of Fraud Prevention, November 1998.
[26] Booth, William, "13 Charged in Gang Importing Prostitutes," The Washington Post, August 21, 1999.
[27] Interview with the Consular Section, American Embassy in Bangkok, February 1999.
[28] Investigative statements resulting from Operation Lost Thai.

Entry Without Inspection

In some trafficking cases, the victims cross into the US without inspection. Latin American "coyotes," commonly used to transport aliens across the southern border, are also used in leading trafficking victims on foot to the US. Vans, buses, and U-haul trucks are also typical modes of transportation. The coyotes' fees generally range from $700 to $1,500 per person.[29]

• One example of this occurred when Mexican traffickers used a coyote to bring women and girls across the border with no documentation. The coyote was paid $700 per individual. According to one of the smuggled individuals, the trip was an arduous journey that required spending 11 days in the hills before crossing on foot. Once in the US, a car took the group to Houston and a van later took them to Florida. The women and girls were then forced into prostitution in Florida and South Carolina.[30]

Traffickers also transit Canada en route to the United States. Organized smuggling rings have capitalized on Canada's visa waiver for Koreans to bring Korean women through Canada to the US where they enter without inspection.[31] Asian traffickers may also use alien smuggling routes to bring their victims into the US.

• In one particularly egregious 1997 trafficking case, a 22 year-old Chinese woman was kidnapped in China, brought to California on a Twainese fishing trawler, and smuggled in with no documentation. In Los Angeles, she was forced to work as a prostitute, confined, raped, and tortured.[32]

Lastly, traffickers also effect entry by booking an international flight for the women that transits an US airport en route to another country. Once in the US airport, the women are met by someone associated with the trafficking ring. The group will then abscond from the airport, purposefully missing their connecting flight.

---

[29] Interview with INS New York, December 1998.
[30] Interview with a trafficker, West Palm Beach, Florida, April 1999.

[31] Cable from the American Embassy in Seoul, 001173, February 23, 1999.
[32] Interview with the AUSA's office, Los Angeles, February 1999.

Intentionally Left Blank

V. Routes To and Within the US

Traffickers move women and children into the United States using a variety of ports of entry. Major ports of entry are Los Angeles' LAX, New York's JFK, Miami International, Chicago's O'Hare, and the San Francisco International Airport. Not coincidentally, Los Angeles, New York, and Miami also rank as the top three cities in the US with the largest problems with visa fraud, according to a consular officer at the State Department's Fraud Prevention office.

Newly emerging hubs of entry include Atlanta, Cleveland, Houston, Orlando, and Washington Dulles.[33] Atlanta's airport, for example, was chosen as the sole entry point for a Thai trafficker who brought in some 90 women during 1994 and 1995. He selected Atlanta because the city was then preparing for the Olympics and he believed the Thai women would blend in with the multitude of ethnic nationalities that were arriving during that period. Additionally, Atlanta was attractive because of the low number of Asian ethnic immigration officials working there.[34]

Other traffickers have flown into Toronto and Vancouver and transported the women overland into the US.[35] Toronto is a popular transit point with the Russians as there are well over 150,000 Russians living there.[36] Traffickers also use Guam and Saipan, two islands in the Commonwealth of the Northern Marianas (CNMI)—a US territory—as a conveyance point since they do not require visas for Koreans. Many ethnically-Korean Chinese women are also trafficked to the Northern Mariana Islands, after having been duped into believing it is easy access to the US or deceived into thinking it was solely a transit point for their onward journey to the US mainland. Once in CNMI, these women are forced to provide sexual services for men in nightclubs and/or work in slave-like conditions in sweatshops.[37, 38]

Once inside the United States, women trafficked for the sex industry may be moved around on an internal circuit that include several of the following cities: New York, Miami, Las Vegas, Houston, Reno, Seattle, Los Angeles, and San Francisco.[39, 40] Experts in the field disagree over whether the movement among these circuits is formally organized or not, but it is clear that the movement of the women among the brothels depends upon the relationship of the brokers and brothel operators, and the various brothels' needs. Typically, the traffickers house the women at staging points until the brothel owners are ready for them.

• For example, in a 1994 trafficking operation, Thai traffickers used several staging areas in New York's Chinatown, Brooklyn, and Connecticut until the brothels could accommodate them. The women were later shuttled around to various brothels in New York. Some women were also sent to Los Angeles, San Francisco, Dallas, Philadelphia, Charlotte, Connecticut, and Kentucky.[41]

These women are moved around the country for several reasons. The traffickers want to ensure "fresh faces" for the clients as well as keep the trafficking victims disoriented so they will not figure out how to contact law enforcement. Additionally, the traffickers move

---

[33] Central Intelligence Agency briefing, Global Trafficking in Women and Children: Assessing the Magnitude, April 1999.
[34] Investigative statements resulting from Operation Lost Thai.
[35] Interview with INS, Bangkok, Thailand, February 1999.
[36] Interview with the Director of Operation Odessa, May 1999.

[37] The Global Survival Network reports that men have also been trafficked to CNMI for sweatshops, construction, and security guard jobs.
[38] Interview with Wellesley College Professor, April 1999.
[39] This list of cities is not an exclusive list.
[40] Interview with California State University, Associate Director Southeast Asian Studies Center, Professor International Studies and Women's Studies, February 1999.
[41] Interview with AUSA and INS, New York, May 1999.

the women to prevent them from developing any sort of relationship with a client who may try and assist them. The time length the women spend at the various brothels varies according to the whims of the traffickers and brothel owners.[42]

• In a trafficking case involving Mexicans, the women and girls were rotated every 15 days among some 11 cities in Florida and two in South Carolina.[43]

• Thai trafficked victims were rotated among 15 to 18 different brothels in the United States from 1994 to 1995. In a similar case involving Asian women, a Thai trafficker rotated Asian women around 20 different brothel houses in 20 different cities. These women were forced to move frequently, and not work at a brothel longer than a month.[44]

Some trafficked victims for other forms of labor, such as peddling trinkets and begging, were also moved around the country. In a second case involving deaf Mexicans, the victims, both female and male, were transported among various US cities, including but not limited to, El Paso, Sanford, Los Angeles, Albuquerque, Tucson, and Phoenix.

[42] Interview with the Department of Justice, Child Exploitation Obscenity Section, September 1998.
[43] Interview with FBI agent, West Palm Beach, Florida, April 1999.

[44] Investigative statements resulting from Operation Lost Thai.

VI. The Traffickers

Trafficking in women is a new business and source of strength for organized crime. Globally, the full spectrum of criminal organizations and shady businesses—from major criminal syndicates to gangs to smuggling rings to loosely associated networks—are involved. Overseas, major organized crime groups, particularly Russian, East European, and Asian syndicates, are heavily involved in trafficking. (Please see Appendix II for further information on organized crime and its involvement in trafficking in women abroad.) In the United States, trafficking in women is primarily being conducted by crime rings and loosely connected criminal networks. In many trafficking cases, the nucleus of these criminal rings is one family or extended family. Additionally, trafficking is perpetrated by a large number of loosely associated crime groups that focus on different aspects of the trafficking process, making detection and crackdowns difficult for law enforcement as the targets are much more amorphous. Though smaller crime groups may be involved in the trafficking industry in the US, this does not diminish the violence that the victims endure, nor does it mean that larger organized crime syndicates will not increasingly become involved in trafficking to the US. Compounding the current threat, law enforcement has also found that the trafficking in women industry is closely intertwined with other related criminal activities, such as extortion, racketeering, money laundering, bribery of public officials, drug use, document forgery, and gambling. Besides extorting from the women, traffickers have also sought to extort from the clients. In some Honolulu brothels, video cameras appear to have been used against the clients. [45]

Asian Criminal Enterprises

The Federal Bureau of Investigation (FBI) reports that Asian criminal enterprises involved in smuggling humans to the US fall into the following categories: 45 percent are Chinese, 29 percent Vietnamese, 7.3 percent Korean with Japanese, Filipino, Thai, Laotian, Cambodian and Polynesian comprising the rest. Asian organized crime organizations have played an intricate part in the smuggling of Asian females to the US and the running of the brothels whether it be as owner, extortionist, or protector. INS investigations have uncovered ties in some cities among the brothels, Asian street gangs, and Asian organized crime figures. Cities where Asian organized crime involvement with brothels has been noted are Los Angeles, San Francisco, Sacramento, Las Vegas, Nevada, and Dallas. INS has also seen Asian street gangs involved with brothels in New York, Philadelphia, and Chicago.

Asian organized crime in the US involved in trafficking in women tends to operate more like a loose confederation of organized criminal entrepreneurs or enterprises as opposed to one large criminal syndicate controlling the trafficking process from beginning to end. Criminal groups are business firms of various sizes depending on their maturity, according to FBI. [46] There tends to be little formal hierarchical organization among Asian organized crime groups. A loose joint venture may cut across ethnic and organizational lines and is often formed for a given opportunity. Trafficking in humans tends to be treated as a business. These criminal enterprises tend to be fairly organized, and will often subcontract

---

[45] Operation Lost Thai Special Report, September 1999.

[46] Federal Bureau of Investigation, Asian Criminal Enterprise Unit, Trafficking of Asian Aliens, July 1998.

out the work. The trafficking-in-persons industry typically involves enforcers, transporters, recruiters, document forgers, brokers, brothel owners, and employment agencies. Brokers operate in the source country as well as in the United States. Thailand is one of the primary source countries for the United States. According to the American Embassy in Bangkok, at least four loosely organized groups smuggle and traffic Thai women for delivery to US brothels. They send roughly 20 to 30 women a month to the US and Canada, generally using altered or impostor Thai passports. By other accounts, at least seven families in Thailand are engaged in smuggling and trafficking women into the United States for prostitution.[47] Many of these women have been told they will be seamstresses and hostesses but arrive to find themselves forced into prostitution. This is often the case with Chinese victims trafficked from rural areas in the PRC. In other cases, Asian women are brought to the US with knowledge of their work as prostitutes, but find themselves in slave-like situations.

Chinese triads and gangs in the US have been involved in alien smuggling and prostitution for years, and increasingly they are arranging for the direct recruiting and smuggling of sex workers from overseas.[48] The Sun Yee On Triad, 14K Triad, Wo Hop To Triad, the United Bamboo Gang, and Fuk Ching Gang are all believed to be involved in alien smuggling to the US, and it is likely that their activities include trafficking. INS Rome has identified over 20 members of Asian organized crime groups who are trafficking and smuggling Asian women and children though Italy to the United States for prostitution and/or pornography. Additionally, an NGO, the Global Survival Network (GSN) found that Chinese criminal groups have moved part of their operations to the Commonwealth of the Northern Mariana Islands (CNMI), where they operate significant money-lending operations which lend money to trafficking victims at exorbitant rates. GSN also found that Japanese organized crime groups operate in Saipan, where they control a large part of the sex tourism sector. Many Chinese women, who have been lured to CNMI to be waitresses, have been forced to work at nightclubs catering to sex tourists and work in sweatshops. Several of these Chinese women have claimed that they were threatened with death if they did not comply.

Brothels across the country generally receive protection from Asian street gangs, who may or may not live at the brothel location. Besides protecting the brothel from other criminal groups, gang members are there to watch over the women until their debt is paid off, according to the FBI. Gang members have also been used to kidnap girls and retrieve those who have escaped. According to one Californian non-governmental organization, the Center for the Pacific-Asian Family, the Vietnamese and Chinese gangs are known to be the most organized and vicious of Asian gangs in California.

• In a New York trafficking case, the brothel owner was forced to pay protection money to the Flying Dragons—a Chinese street gang. The Flying Dragons are the enforcement sector of the Hipsing Triad, a Fukienese Triad. In order to maintain a low profile, the Hipsing Triad is registered under the Hipsing merchants association.[49]

• The Wah Ching and Triads also employ Asian street gangs, such as the Black Dragons and Koolboyz, for protection at the brothels.[50]

---

[47] Investigative statements resulting from Operation Lost Thai.
[48] Bureau of Consular Affairs, Fraud Digest, "More Chinese Women Become trafficking Victims," November/December 1998.

---

[49] Interview with INS, New York, May 1999.
[50] Operation Lost Thai Special Report, September 1999.

- In a 1998 internal trafficking case in California, a Fresno-based gang kidnapped Hmong[51] girls, took them to other cities, and forced them into prostitution.[52]

- A few years ago, some 65 Chinese citizens were held in a Maryland basement while arrangements could be made by their traffickers to sell them to Chinese gangs in New York for servitude in restaurants. The Chinese were also beaten and forced to call their families and ask for more money.[53]

To evade detection from law enforcement, Asian traffickers shift their holding houses on a frequent basis; forbid the women from making prostitution out-calls; accept only Asian clients at the brothels; and use massage parlors, spas, sun tanning parlors, and beauty salons as fronts for the brothels. Many massage parlors in the United States are connected to large-scale smuggling and prostitution operations. Traffickers may purchase false massage licenses or certificates for the women, costing anywhere from $200 to $500, in order to appear legitimate in case a police officer enters the premises. Though many prostitution houses operate independently, they appear to share information with one another regarding any possible law enforcement raids, and some have hideaways to conceal the women and girls from the police.[54] Corruption also facilitates the industry. For example, there have been allegations made against New Orleans police department officials that they were accepting bribes from local brothels, likely in exchange for tipping the brothels off to impending raids.

Russian Crime Groups and Syndicates

All levels of Russian organized crime, from individuals to smaller groups to larger syndicates, appear to be involved in trafficking women to the United States, though law enforcement entities disagree as to the degree of involvement of Russian organized crime. By some accounts, Russian individuals—likely with Russian organized crime connections—are importing women from Russia, Ukraine, the Baltic States, and Central Europe for the sex industry, namely for stripping, escort services, and prostitution. INS agents in New York claim there are many cases involving the trafficking of these women by freelance criminals for stripping or escort services. Frequently, the women's passports are taken by the trafficker and they are not free to leave until they have paid their debt of around $10,000. INS believes these criminals have Russian organized crime connections overseas, but have not seen instances where the major Russian organized crime organizations are running the trafficking business to the United States.

The Director of Operation Odessa, a Florida task force designed to combat Russian organized crime, believes that individual criminals, not necessarily organized crime, are trafficking Russian women to Florida. He claims that women are being trafficked to Miami, Orlando, Fort Lauderdale, Jackson, Palm Beach, and increasingly the Florida panhandle. In his opinion, Russian entrepreneurs, with ties to Russian organized crime, are importing women for Florida's sex industry. For example, one Russian, Sergey Skobeltsyn, with alleged ties to the Russian organized crime group Kazanskaya, bought two strip clubs, Pure Platinum and Solid Gold, for $8 million dollars in late 1996.[55] And Ludwig Fainberg, a Russian mafia figure with alleged ties to Colombian drug traffickers, was also

---

[51] An indigenous hill tr be refugee population from Indochina.
[52] Interview with Little Tokyo Service Center, Los Angeles, California, February 1999.
[53] Interview with INS, Washington, DC, July 1999.
[54] Investigative statements resulting from Operation Lost Thai.

---

[55] Interview with AUSA Fort Lauderdale, Florida, May 1999.

heavily involved in running a strip club called Porkys, which likely involved trafficked women. FBI headquarters also has information that the following major Russian organized crime syndicates—the Izmailovskaya, Dagestantsy, Kazanskaya, and Solntsenskaya—are involved in the prostitution industry throughout the United States. Given the way these organized crime syndicates operate overseas and the brutality of these organizations, it is likely that this involvement in the US includes trafficking in women through the use of deception, threats, and violence.

Russian women have also been trafficked to Florida, particularly the panhandle, for maid work.[56] FBI and INS agents in Florida claim that Russian and Central European women are answering ads in local papers for work in the US. Once in the US, these women provide maid service in motels and become virtual indentured servants, working long hours for little pay. The women are paid through a series of corporations so the women appear to be working only part-time and so the companies do not need to provide any benefits. FBI is unsure as to whether or not any larger Russian criminal syndicate is managing these companies.

Another interesting trend identified by FBI agents in New York are situations where local Russian organized crime groups tried to "muscle in" and control a trafficking situation after they have noticed its profitability. Bratva— the Brotherhood—a Russian crime group with ties to Russian crime boss Ivankov's successor organization—used extortion, assault, and battery in July 1998 to control dance agencies and their drivers who were bringing Russian women in and delivering them to exotic nightclubs, bars, and escort services. FBI believes there are about 10 to 12 dance agencies specializing in Russian women, and hundreds of escort services in the

New York and New Jersey area. Each dance agency is believed to employ some 60 to 200 women. Again, it is not readily apparent to FBI to what degree Russian organized crime is involved in controlling these 10 to 12 New York and New Jersey dance agencies.

Some Diplomatic Security (DS) agents claim that many of these dance, modeling, employment, or service agencies are fronts for trafficking for larger Russian organized crime syndicates. According to these DS agents, the agencies are used to hide the structural layers of the criminal organization, which include deputies, associates, collectors, and drivers. They claim that Russian and Italian organized crime groups are collaborating in New York and New Jersey with Russian crime groups supplying the women for the multitude of nightclubs and peep shows that are managed by Italian mafia groups.

In other instances, traffickers have capitalized on the reputation of Russian organized crime and used it as a means of control and intimidation. In a recent Chicago case, a Russian American frequently bragged about his Chechen organized crime ties and threatened Latvian women with harm to themselves and/or their families if they did not dance nude. He had originally intimidated one of the women into coming to the US, by telling her he would cut her face up if she refused and then escorting her to a mafia hangout for dinner so she would know that her face had been identified.[57]

Threats, such as these, have been carried out in other instances. In one case, a Russian woman was brought over to be a maid but forced into prostitution to repay her smuggling debt more quickly. When this woman tried to leave, a Russian thug beat her so badly she had to go to the hospital where she was threatened by another Russian gangster not to talk to law enforcement officials.[58] In another

[56] Interview with the Director of Operation Odessa, May 1999.

[57] Interview, the AUSA's Office, Chicago, July 1999.

case, the authorities suspected mafia involvement in the gruesome murder of a Russian woman trafficked to Maryland. The case was never solved, but some authorities think she was killed because she was holding back her earnings from her employers.[59]

Latin American Traffickers

In general, there is less information about the Latin American crime groups that traffic in women, though this does not necessarily mean that they are any less involved in trafficking. It appears that they operate in some similar ways to Asian traffickers as Latin traffickers have been noted using independent contractors to move trafficking victims across the border, and transport them farther inside the US interior.[60] Latin American traffickers appear to use similar routes and means used in alien smuggling operations. It is likely that corruption facilitates trafficking operations, similar to alien smuggling. Human smugglers allegedly pay bribes ranging from $200 to $500 dollars to officials from Grupo Beta, the state judicial police and municipal police. The consequence for not paying a bribe can result in jail time from two to three days and the distribution of aliens to other smugglers for roughly $50.[61]

In order to evade detection, Latin traffickers vary their routes once law enforcement has developed "profiles" for their victims. Moreover, these traffickers try to insulate themselves by victimizing those within their own ethnic group and by controlling the clientele that frequent their underground brothels. For example, Mexican and other Latin American brothel owners will generally only permit other Latinos into the brothels.[62]

---

[58] Interview with the Director of Operation Odessa, May 1999.
[59] Interview with INS, Washington, DC, July 1999.
[60] Interview with INS, Washington, DC, 1999.

[61] Cable from the American consulate in Tijuana 0698, June 1999.
[62] Interview with Department of Justice, Civil Rights Division, Criminal Section, April 1999.

Intentionally Left Blank

VII. Profits from the Industry

Profits in the trafficking industry provide a major source of income for the crime rings. In most of the major recent trafficking cases in the United States, the traffickers made anywhere from one to eight million in a period ranging from one to six years.[63]

Traffickers typically charge the women inflated prices for securing the alleged jobs, travel documentation, transportation, lodging, meals, and incidentals. To increase profits, the women are kept in poor, crowded conditions. It is also common for trafficked women to be charged to buy their passport back. The fee is usually around $900 for women from the Newly Independent States and Central Europe,[64] though in one recent case in Chicago, Latvian women paid as much as $4,000 in cash.[65, 66] Trafficked Asian women have been charged $1,500 to $3,000 for their passports. Women may also be charged for ID cards, driver's licenses, and driver's permits. Prices may vary, but typical fees are $700 for an ID card, $900 for a driver's license and $1,000 for an ID card with a driver's permit.[67]

It is illustrative to examine fees from one case involving an Asian trafficker that appears characteristic for other Asian traffickers. In this case, a Thai smuggler is paid between $13,000 to $15,000 for every successful entry a woman made into the US. The money covers the passport (typically sold for $1,500 to $3,000), airline ticket, and additional fees paid to the Thai recruiting agent and the "jockey" who assists in bringing the women into the United States. Thai recruitment agents receive a commission of about $800 to $1,400 for each woman he or she recruited. The "jockey," or person who actually escorts a woman or girl

from Thailand to the US, is usually paid about $1,000 per woman or girl he successfully admits to the US. Thus, the smuggler usually makes about $7,500 to $9,000 per woman.[68]

Traffickers have also come up with various means to transport the money back to Thailand and the agents. The "jockey" may be responsible for conveying the impostor passport and the $13,000 back to the Thai smuggler in Thailand. Alternatively, the money is wired through companies to Thai bank accounts.

Overall profits in the trade can be staggering, as several cases indicate. Thai traffickers, who incarcerated Thai women and men in a sweatshop in El Monte, California, are estimated to have made $8 million dollars over about six years.[69]

• Thai traffickers, who enslaved Thai women in a New York brothel, made about $1.5 million over roughly a year and three months. In that case, the women were made to pay debts ranging from $30,000 to $50,000. The women were forced to charge $130 per client; the madam of the brothel would receive $30 and the smugglers would receive $100. Sometimes, a woman at the brothel might be sold outright to the madam for $15,000 or more depending on her beauty.[70, 71]

• One Thai trafficker estimates that he made about $215,000 over approximately two years. In this case as well, brothel owners would pay $7,500 to $15,000 for each woman, though her debt would be around $40,000. Less attractive women would be exchanged or sold off for less money.[72]

---

[63] Restitution, when ordered for the trafficking victims, generally fell far short of the traffickers' profits.
[64] Interview with FBI, New York, December 1998.
[65] The traffickers had initially offered to sell the Latvian women their passports for up to $60,000.
[66] Interview with the AUSA's office Chicago, July 1999.
[67] Investigative statements resulting from Operation Lost Thai.

[68] Investigative statements resulting from Operation Lost Thai.
[69] Interview with INS, Los Angeles, February 1999.
[70] In these cases, the woman would be indebted to the brothel madam, not the smuggler.
[71] Interview with INS and the AUSA's office, New York, May 1999.

- Chinese criminal syndicates, living in Malaysia, have also made $5,000 to $7,000 for each Malaysian woman delivered to the United States, according to the American Embassy in Kuala Lumpur. A kidnapped and trafficked Chinese woman in yet another case was compelled to pay a $20,000 debt through prostitution.[73]

Profits from trafficking women from Latin America can be just as lucrative. A Mexican crime family, that forced deaf Mexicans to peddle trinkets made roughly $8 million, over four and a half years.[74]

In another trafficking case involving Mexicans, traffickers made some $2.5 million over two years by forcing Mexican women and girls into prostitution. The traffickers charged a client $22 for 15 minutes of sexual activity with a woman. Ten dollars of this amount went to the house and the remainder towards paying off her $2,000 to $3,000 debt. The traffickers then used the money to buy real estate and new trucks in Mexico. These assets were used to convince additional victims that they were successful businessmen who owned a legitimate landscaping company in the US[75]

---

[72] Investigative statements resulting from Operation Lost Thai.
[73] Interview with the AUSA's office, Los Angeles, February 1999.
[74] Interview with the Department of Justice's Civil Rights Division, Criminal Section, April 1999.

[75] Interview with the Department of Justice's Civil Rights Division, Criminal Section, April 1999.
and Interview with FBI agent, West Palm Beach, Florida, April 1999.

VIII. Trafficking In Children

Trafficking in women is much more extensive in the United States than is trafficking in children; however, trafficking in minors appears to be a growing issue. The extent of the problem is difficult to document, but numerous investigations suggest trafficking in minors for the sex or labor industry is common.

For the Sex Industry

Trafficking in teenage girls for the sex industry is occurring throughout the US. For example, from February 1996 to about March 1998, some 25 to 40 Mexican women and girls—some as young as 14 years old—were trafficked to Florida and South Carolina for prostitution. The traffickers had promised the girls good jobs in landscaping, childcare, and elder care, and worked to convince their parents that the jobs were legitimate.[76] In a different investigation, an INS agent in New York reports that Mexicans are trafficking Mexican teenagers into California and bringing them to New York for prostitution. Some of the teens know they will be prostitutes, while others are duped.

The FBI reports that Asian girls have also been discovered in forced prostitution cases. In August, an organized crime task force in Atlanta, indicted 13 members of an Asian smuggling ring for trafficking up to 1,000 Asian women and girls, between the ages of 13 and 25, to Atlanta and other US cities for prostitution. The women and girls were held in bondage until their $30,000 to $40,000 contracts were paid off. One brothel was described by law enforcement as a "prison compound" with barbed wire, fences, chained dogs, and gang members who served as guards.[77]

Additionally, the Coalition Against Trafficking in Women has reported that operators of the Hong Kong Spa in Washington, DC were arrested in 1995 for purchasing underage immigrant Asian girls, one only 13 years old, in Atlantic City and transporting them to DC to work in an indentured sexual servitude arrangement. The girls had answered ads in local newspapers for restaurant jobs paying $1,000 to $2,700 a week but were picked up at the airport and taken to massage parlors and brothels and forced to work up to 15 hours a day. The NGO, "End Child Prostitution, Child Pornography, and Trafficking in Children for Sexual Purposes," claims that the recent Asian economic crisis has made Asian children particularly vulnerable to traffickers as more and more children are dropping out of school to look for work to support their families.[78]

In Vancouver, British Columbia, an INS investigator in Vancouver reports that a group of American Canadian pimps, calling themselves the West Coast Players, are actively involved in trafficking Canadian teenagers to Los Angeles for the sex industry. There are indications that the West Coast Players are establishing links with Asian organized crime groups in British Columbia. Canadian law enforcement officials also believe that American girls are also being trafficked from the US to Canada.[79] In 1998, a pimp and his co-defendants were convicted in DC on eight counts of transporting minors from Canada across the US-Canadian border and across state lines for prostitution.

Children have also been trafficked internally within the United States. The NGO the Little Tokyo Service Center reports that in 1998 in northern California, a Hmong gang kidnapped, raped, and forced into prostitution Hmong girls.

---

[76] Interview with FBI agent, West Palm Beach, Florida, April 1999.
[77] Booth, William, "13 Charged in Gang Importing Prostitutes," The Washington Post, August 21, 1999.

[78] "Impact of the Asian Financial Economic Crisis on Child Prostitution," End Child Prostitution, Child Pornography, and Trafficking in Children for Sexual Purposes," Newsletter, May 1999.
[79] Cable from the American Consulate, Vancouver, 1080, September 18, 1998.

There were roughly 15 girls, ages 13 to 15, whom were trafficked to other cities and forced to submit to sexual slavery for members of their own ethnic community.[80] Even more recently in October, four teenage Hmong girls were lured to Detroit by Hmong men and boys where they were allegedly gang raped, assaulted, and threatened with death if they tried to escape.[81] The Department of Justice's Child Exploitation and Obscenity Section cites at least nine other domestic cases from 1997 to 1998 in which minors were trafficked internally for prostitution.[82]

Also within the United States, experts at the National Center for Missing and Exploited Children claim that outlaw American motorcycle gangs used to be heavily involved in befriending, pimping, and trafficking vulnerable youths and runaways some fifteen years ago. These gangs moved the minors around the country, passing them off from one pimp or brothel to the next. In some cases, the girls were transported along a "sports circuit," moving from the Kentucky Derby to the Preakness to the Indi 500 and so on. The Center has not seen any incidences of outlaw motorcycle gang involvement in trafficking girls over the last several years.

For the Labor Industry

Trafficking in children for other labor sectors is also happening, though it is difficult to determine the magnitude of the problem. African and Middle Eastern families, for example, are bringing over children to work as domestics. They typically bring the child to the United States, claiming the child is their niece or nephew. The child is then made to work long hours and perform hard work under dangerous conditions. There are cases where the young domestics have been made to scour bathrooms daily with noxious cleaning chemicals.[83]

• A Floridian family was recently taken into custody for forcing a 12-year-old girl, brought from Haiti, to be a maid and repeatedly assaulting her.[84]

• In New York, a Nigerian smuggling ring is charging parents $10,000 to $20,000 to bring their children to the US, promising the parents that their children will have better educational opportunities. Once in the US, the ring forces the Nigerian children to work as domestics.[85]

• From February 1997 to August 1998 in Woodbine, Maryland, a pastor was bringing in Estonian children, ages 14 to 17, promising them they would attend Calvary Chapel Christian Academy but then forcing them to clean roach-infested apartments and install office furniture. The children were working 15 hours a day and being paid about $10 to $50 a week. Some children were threatened that they would be sent home if they refused, and punishments included skipping meals and standing in one spot for prolonged periods.[86]

• INS has also worked on cases involving South Asian children smuggled into the US to work at low wage scale jobs. In one case, about 100 Indian children, some as young as

[80] Interview with the Little Tokyo Service Center, February 1999 and Associated Press, "Police Break Up Sex-Slave Ring That Preyed On Immigrant Girls," November 13, 1998.
[81] Associated Press, "Rape Allegations Shake Hmong Refugees," October 14, 1999.
[82] These cases include: US v. Howard Draper, US v. Vernon Miller, US v. Troy Footman, US v. Andre and Jerome Young, US v. Jon Cureton and Daunya Richfield, US v. Courtney Fitzgerald and Shannon Brooks, US v. Omar Ross, US v. William Clark, US v. Brandon Wright.

[83] Interview with the Department of Justice, Civil Rights Division, Criminal Section, April 1999.
[84] "Haitian Girl Illegally Residing in the US, Sexually Abused and Forced to be a Maid," Miami Herald, September 30, 1999.
[85] Interview with INS, Washington, DC, July 1999.
[86] Interview with INS, Baltimore, July 1999, and AP, Baltimore, July 27, 1999.

9 or 10, were being brought into New York from 1996 to 1997 and shuffled around the country to work in construction and restaurants. Some of the children appeared to have been sold by their parents to the traffickers. [87]

---

[87] Interview with INS, Baltimore, July 1999.

Intentionally Left Blank

IX. Criminal Exploitation of Women Brought to the US—A Broad Spectrum

In the United States, criminal exploitation of women brought to the US encompasses a variety of cases that fall along a continuum of exploitation and abuse. On one end of the continuum are trafficking cases, characterized by slavery or slavery-like treatment of the trafficking victims. On the other end is the criminal exploitation of smuggled economic migrants including fair labor and safety standard violations. While cases on either end are quite distinctive, some cases in the middle of the continuum are less clear-cut. It may be harder to conclude definitively whether or not they are trafficking cases. In practice, these evaluations must be made on a case-by-case basis. The government seeks to address all types of exploitation, though the types of protection and assistance afforded the victims differ depending upon where the victims fall within the spectrum.

The most egregious trafficking cases tend to make the headlines and involve the worst cases of involuntary servitude, violence, and human rights abuses. In these cases, women may be forced to work anywhere from sixteen to twenty hours per day, and often live in conditions of captivity within the US. These women have had their freedoms severely curtailed. They are kept in situations of forced labor through sexual, physical, and psychological abuse; threats of violence to themselves and/or their families; bonded labor; enforced isolation; and/or seizure of their passports, travel, or identity documents. Human rights abuses in the worst cases that have been uncovered have included: forcing minors into prostitution; confining a teenager in a closet for two weeks as punishment for attempting to escape; compelling an adult female to wear a dog collar and sleep with the dogs; torturing a young victim with cigarette burns; and using a stun gun for punishment on a deaf person. In one Dallas brothel, Thai nationals were locked up and forced to work as prostitutes. They were treated like animals in that if they did not do as they were told, they would not receive any food. Cases, in

particular, that involve organized crime elements tend to receive the greatest amount of attention. Fortunately, long-term and large-scale organized bondage is the rarest kind of involuntary servitude in the United States, though it continues to occur. There are also fewer slave sharecropping and less African-American slave labor crews being reported or discovered in the US.[88] The violent subjugation under labor crew bosses, that was common 15 years ago, appears to be less prevalent now.[89]

As we move away from the unambiguous instances of trafficking, cases may not fit as neatly into definitional boxes. There are a variety of cases that might not be straight trafficking cases, but involve strong trafficking elements, such as the use of psychological manipulation and the seizure of identity papers, both of which are very common. The confiscation of identity papers, particularly for women from the former Soviet bloc, can be particularly frightening for these women and a very real means of control. Frequently, women trafficked to the United States are aware of the job but unaware of the abusive conditions they ultimately find themselves in. The women arrive in the United States and find that their debt or the terms of repayment have changed considerably. In addition to being charged for the cost of their travel and for traffickers' commissions, they are charged exorbitant or inflated amounts for room and board and other basic necessities, such as clothing and medicines. The traffickers usually engage in irregular accounting practices and charge the women usurious interest rates. In these cases, the traffickers frequently change their tactics in an effort to keep the women a little "off balance;" for example, sometimes the women must be accompanied when they leave the premises, sometimes they are permitted to do errands unescorted. Victims' attorneys have

---

[88] Interview with Department of Justice, Civil Rights Division, Criminal Section, April 1999.
[89] Navarro, Mireya, "Case of Florida Au Pair Reflects Wider Problem," The New York Times, December 12, 1996: A-12.

also said that while the traffickers might not have beaten their clients, these women had witnessed the traffickers hitting their girlfriends and therefore did not want to risk making the traffickers angry.

Farther down the spectrum, many economic migrants have been severely exploited. Largely uneducated and heavily indebted to the smuggling rings, some illegal aliens are encouraged to sell drugs or go into prostitution to repay their debt. Aliens, with little to no formal education, are sometimes urged to sign contracts, which they cannot understand and commit them to working with hazardous chemicals. Many illegal migrants, who work on agricultural farms, find themselves working long hours and under difficult, precarious conditions. Inflated costs for meals, lodging, and incidentals ensure the migrants never repay their debt.

X. Related Industries

Closely linked in public perception to trafficking in women are a variety of profitable businesses and fraud schemes that entail the exploitation of foreign women, such as unlicensed mail order bride companies, maid schemes, and domestic servants. Typically, women know they are going to the US for marriage or maid services, but they are abused or exploited once in the US. Many exploitation cases involving domestic workers are particularly hard cases to document because of the privacy afforded by a home.[90] Trafficking may be occurring in some or possibly all of these situations, though this would have to be judged on a case by case basis. Mail order bride brokers, for example, are not traffickers per se; but, where there is deception or fraudulent non-disclosure of known facts concerning the nature of the relationship being entered into or the criminal or abusive background of the client, the brokers should be liable as traffickers.[91]

Mail Order Bride Companies

Foreign women and American men are increasingly using marriage or international matchmaking agencies, services, or "mail order bride" catalogues to find a spouse. While international matchmaking agencies are considered legitimate businesses, they are almost completely unregulated.[92] There is generally no obligation for full disclosure, no liability, and no obligation to give the women information about their rights. A non-governmental organization, the Global Survival Network (GSN); found that marriage agencies generally do not screen their male clients, some of whom have histories of

domestic violence or criminal records. Another consequence of the lack of regulation is that marriage agencies are able to advertise minors. In March 1999, the INS reported that the number of mail-order bride agencies in the US was growing rapidly. It reported that there were over 200 mail order bride agencies operating in the US in 1998. These agencies are bringing approximately 4,000 to 6,000 women, mostly from the Philippines or the Newly Independent States, to the US each year.[93] GSN also reports that most of the matchmaking companies in Russia have links to Russian organized crime. These ties facilitate trafficking, as GSN found the Russian mafia recruits women at mixers or matchmaking parties, organized by marriage agencies. Russian organized crime is also using these companies' databases to get additional names of possible recruits who wish to marry and/or work abroad.

Maid Schemes

Another industry that may front for some trafficking cases is maid schemes that are used to supply émigré families in the US with a steady stream of domestic workers, usually women between the ages of 35 and 55 years old. Typically, the women come in on B-1 or B-2 visas where a member of the fraud ring meets them at the airport. The women are then taken to a "safe house," their documents are seized, and they are later placed with a family. Often the terms of employment are not what the women were led to expect. Many of the women are forced to work long hours for little pay. They are usually not paid directly, but rather their salaries are given to a placement organization that gives them a percentage. Women who complain have been kept in line by threats, intimidation, and/or physical violence.[94]

[90] Navarro, "Case of Florida Au Pair Reflects Wider Problem," A-12.
[91] Miller, Ali and Stewart, Alison, Report from the Roundtable on The Meaning of Trafficking in Persons: A Human Rights Perspective, Women's Rights Law Reporter, Rutgers Law School Fall/Winter 1998.
[92] Global Survival Network, "Crime and Servitude: An Expose of the Traffic in Women for Prostitution from the Newly Independent States," October 1997.

[93] Hughes, Donna, "Pimps and Predators on the Internet," The Coalition Against Trafficking in Women, March 1999.

Domestic Servants

Lately, several cases have come to light involving foreign women being exploited as domestic servants for foreign diplomats or other officials at international financial institutions. Many former domestic servants claim that they found themselves in situations akin to slavery or bonded servitude. They reported that their employers confiscated their passports and other documents, required dusk to dawn labor for little or sometimes no pay, and forbid them from leaving the house or making contact with other domestic workers.[95]

- For example, an illiterate Ethiopian woman was brought to the United States eight years ago by an IMF staff member to work as a maid. She was made to work seven days a week 15 hours a day, isolated from others, and physically abused. Though promised $235 a week plus medical care, she received less than 3 cents an hour.[96]

- In another case, a nanny from the Philippines was brought into the US to work for Philippine embassy employees, but then sent to work for another family for 41 cents an hour, 16 hours a day.

According to the State Department, 3,800 domestic servants come to the US each year under two types of temporary employment visas to work for foreign diplomats or non-US staff members of international organizations. These employers are to abide by US labor laws, but a fellow at the Institute for Policy Studies claims that there is no monitoring by the World Bank or IMF to ensure that staff members meet their obligations.[97] The Global Survival Network concurs that there is no effective monitoring of domestic workers who are brought into the United States to work for diplomats and officials of international agencies.

Illicit Foreign Adoptions

The buying and selling of babies under the guise of an adoption is yet another extension of trafficking and an egregious human rights violation. In the case of foreign adoption, several means of procurement have been identified to secure the babies. Smuggling rings might pay rural midwives to falsely register the birth of a child under a woman's name. A child is then stolen from its family and given to the falsely registered mother who then gives the child up for adoption. Alternatively, trafficking networks have been known to procure children by drugging or tricking uneducated mothers into "thumb-printing" a blank legal document.[98, 99] Shady adoption agencies have also worked to convince impoverished parents to give up their baby so it will be given a much "better life" in the US. Concerned by these unlawful and unscrupulous tactics, the Guatemalan government invited last July the UN representative for the Sale of Children, Child Prostitution and Pornography to Guatemala to evaluate the situation of the sale of children in the country.[100]

Illicit adoptions have also occurred in Mexico and other parts of Central America. In July, two American women and a Mexican lawyer were

---

[94] "The Russian Maid Scheme," Department of State, Bureau of Consular Affairs, Office of Fraud, Prevention Programs, August 1997.

[95] "Not in This Country, They Can't," Editorial, The Washington Post, January 7, 1999: A24.

[96] Branigin, William, "A Life of Exhaustion, Beatings and Isolation," The Washington Post, January 5, 1999.

[97] Branigin, William, "Modern-Day Slavery, Imported Servants Allege Abuse By Foreign Host Families in US," The Washington Post, January 5, 1999, A1.

[98] This occurred in Guatemala that is the fourth-largest source of children for US adoptions, behind Russia, China, and South Korea.

[99] Bird, Yoshi, "The Trafficking of Children for Sexual Exploitation and Foreign Adoption: Background and Current Measures," Draft document, International Criminal Police Organization (INTERPOL), August 1999.

[100] "UN Representative to Travel to Guatemala to Assess Sale of Children," Mercyhurst, July 13, 1999.

charged with taking part in an illegal adoption ring in which 17 Mexican babies were smuggled across the border and placed in American homes for approximately $22,000 each. The ring used Mexican women with legal border-crossing documents to pose as mothers to escort the children from Mexico into the US. In another case in El Salvador, police arrested in May the ringleader of a major criminal organization that specialized in smuggling children into the US. The ringleader had been paying corrupt civil registry officials to provide false birth certificates.[101]

---

[101] Associated Press, "Adoptions of Smuggled Mexican Babies," July 25, 1999.

Intentionally Left Blank

XI. Issues and Challenges Associated with Combating Trafficking

After interviewing over 150 individuals in the public and private sector on the trafficking issue, it is clear that uncovering, investigating, and prosecuting trafficking in women cases while protecting, assisting, and repatriating trafficking victims is a complicated and resource-intensive task. Individuals within the Departments of Justice, State, Treasury, and Labor, the Intelligence Community, state and local police, as well as non-governmental organizations, academic institutions, and foreign governments all identified their most pressing concerns and difficulties in combating the traffickers and/or protecting the victims. [102]

Definitional, Information-Sharing, and Coordination Difficulties

Definitional difficulties still persist regarding trafficking in women. Different branches of the government and various offices within those branches frequently define, categorize, and handle trafficking cases in different ways. Distinctions regarding trafficking in women, alien smuggling, and irregular migration are sometimes blurred with INS predisposed to jump to the conclusion that most cases involving illegal workers are alien smuggling instead of trafficking cases. One INS agent recently stated that there are no innocent victims, they are all willing participants. Consequently, their focus is on deporting the women once they are discovered. Less emphasis is placed on the exploitative settings these women find themselves in. Additionally, the Department of Justice sometimes tabulates or labels trafficking cases as worker exploitation cases. The label suggests

something closer to wage and hour problems versus involuntary servitude, debt bondage, and forced prostitution.

In an effort to bolster information sharing and coordination at the federal, regional, state, and local levels, the Attorney General created the Worker Exploitation Task Force in April 1998. This Task Force created a manual on Investigating and Prosecuting Worker Exploitation and Abuse Cases and is holding training programs for local, state, and federal law enforcement on worker exploitation. Nonetheless, information sharing among the various entities remains imperfect. Several Department of Justice offices look at the trafficking issue through the prism of their particular office's interest, be it eliminating civil rights violations, tackling organized crime, or protecting minors. Even within the Department of Justice, information is not always shared among the concerned offices. Moreover, case information is often kept at the field offices. Many FBI agents say it is difficult, if not impossible, to formally write-up the cases and lessons learned once they are completed given their demanding workload, inadequate staffing, and pressing new cases. Furthermore, there is no one central repository of all the trafficking in women and children cases within the United States.

Information sharing and coordination with overseas law enforcement entities is also often burdensome. One Assistant US Attorney from New York claims coordination with foreign law enforcement agencies is problematic given extensive corruption within those bodies. Bureaucratic infighting, overlapping and unclear responsibilities among foreign law enforcement bodies, and a lack of clarity over what information can be disclosed to US officials makes prosecuting foreign traffickers particularly challenging. Though Interpol's main offices try to expedite communication among national police forces of countries in which trafficking in persons is a problem, member countries are slow to report cases of

---

[102] A compilation of a variety of perspectives is outlined below. Thoughts are not attributed to specific individuals in order that a more frank and candid discussion could ensue about the real issues facing law enforcement and so that this trafficking report could be unclassified. Additionally, the views expressed are individual opinions; they do not necessarily represent the views of their offices or bureaus.

suspected trafficking in women to Interpol as well as to exchange relevant trafficking information amongst themselves.[103]

Investigative Challenges

There are many challenges facing law enforcement that hampers its ability to combat trafficking. Limited resources hinder law enforcement's ability to investigate and prosecute trafficking cases. For instance, at the same time the Department of Justice's Civil Rights Division is intensifying its efforts to prosecute trafficking cases, its responsibilities are growing in the areas of police brutality, hate crimes, church burnings, and abortion clinic violence, without an equivalent increase in funding or resources. According to a federal prosecutor who works on slavery cases, investigating trafficking and slavery cases is also arduous, as it is extremely difficult to infiltrate many ethnic crime groups that are engaged in trafficking. This prosecutor believes the FBI needs more ethnic Chinese or Spanish-speaking agents, especially ones familiar with particular dialects. In the Latin American immigrant community, for example, there are a lot of important language subtleties, specific dialects, and cultural mannerisms which agents have a hard time mimicking. Even Spanish and English varies according to how long the immigrant trafficker has been in the US. The multitude of Asian languages also makes it hard for law enforcement to go undercover. The benefit of having an agent speak Thai was demonstrated in Los Angeles when INS was investigating the El Monte slave labor case involving over 70 Thai victims.

Law enforcement also has few resources to hire and train ethnic female officers for trafficking undercover work. Even if they did

have the resources, federal prosecutors have noted that it is nearly impossible to use a female undercover agent because she would have to be a victim. In order to prove slavery, beatings, and forced prostitution, she would risk suffering these traumas. This contrasts with infiltrating a drug operation, in which the agent's undercover responsibilities might include buying, selling, or transporting drugs from one location to the next.

Another investigative challenge is that many law enforcement officials do not hear about trafficking cases or receive lead information. Having been threatened by the traffickers, many trafficking victims either are unable to or fearful of coming forward. Additionally, traffickers have usually supplied the women with answers and statements they should tell law enforcement if they are caught. Victims often distrust law enforcement as the traffickers have played upon their concerns of law enforcement in their own countries. Furthermore, victims almost always fear deportation. These same anxieties sometimes make victims reluctant to testify in a trial. Despite being victimized, they feel ashamed and overwhelmed by the lengthy ordeal of a trial. At times, conflicting statements from victims makes law enforcement's job of building a case more challenging.

Thus, law enforcement may at times have to rely on other investigative techniques such as tapping the traffickers' phones. Some prosecutors, however, feel handicapped and would like broader discretion in being able to use Title 3, the wire statute. In particular, one Assistant US Attorney from Miami said that the Mann Act—transportation for illegal sexual activity—should be used as a predicate offense for Title 3.

Additionally, proving trafficking and involuntary servitude cases is difficult, as the prosecutor must often demonstrate that force or the threat of force was used to intimidate the trafficking victims. An Assistant US Attorney from

---

[103] Bird, Yoshi, "The Challenges Posed By Insufficient Collaboration and Communication in the Pro-Active Fight Against Trafficking of Women," Interpol, September 1999.

Los Angeles, who has worked on trafficking cases, claims that the force is often psychological rather than physical, and harder to prove as it is generally the woman's word against the traffickers.

Low Penalties for the Traffickers

A review of the trafficking cases shows that the penalties appear light, especially when compared to sentences given to drug dealers, and do not appear to reflect the multitude of human rights abuses perpetrated against the women. The statutory maximum[104] for sale into involuntary servitude is only ten years per count, whereas the statutory maximum for dealing in ten grams of LSD or distributing a kilo of heroin is life. At the state level, in Maryland for example, a defendant convicted of a felony drug charge, who has two prior misdemeanor drug charges, would be required to serve ten years without the possibility of parole. Thus, the perception is that punishment for trafficking in women is less than or equal to the punishment for trafficking in drugs. Even small amounts of drugs can carry tough sentences. At present, a defendant convicted of dealing at least five grams of crack cocaine in the federal system receives a mandatory **minimum** sentence of five years. Additionally, sentencing enhancements for use of a gun during the commission of a violent crime or drug trafficking is five years mandatory for the first offense and then 20 years for each subsequent violation.

- In Los Angeles, where traffickers kidnapped a Chinese woman, raped her, forced her into prostitution, posted guards to control her movements, and burned her with cigarettes, the lead defendant received four years and the other defendants received two to three years.[105]

- In another case where Asian women were kept physically confined for years with metal bars on the windows, guards, and an electronic monitoring system and were forced to submit to sex with as many as 400 customers to repay their smuggling debt, the traffickers received between four and nine years.[106]

- In a case involving some 70 deaf Mexicans who were held under lock and key, forced to peddle trinkets, beaten, and in some cases tortured, the ringleader received 14 years and the other traffickers received from 1 to 8 years.

- In a 1996 trafficking case involving Russian and Ukrainian women, who had answered ads to be au pairs, sales clerks, and waitresses, but were forced to provide sexual services and live in a massage parlor in Bethesda, Maryland, the Russian-American massage parlor owner was fined. He entered a plea bargain and charges were dropped with the restriction that he would not operate a business again in Montgomery County.[107] The women, who had not been paid any salary and were charged $150 dollars for their housing, were deported or left the US voluntarily.

- In a trafficking case involving over 70 Thai laborers who had been held against their will, systematically abused, and made to work 20-hour shifts in a sweatshop, the seven defendants received sentences ranging from four to seven years, with one defendant receiving seven months.

- In a trafficking case involving forced prostitution, confinement, assault, rape, and forced abortions, sixteen defendants were charged with a variety of Title 18 and Title 8 offenses ranging from involuntary servitude

---

[104] The statutory maximum sets forth the outer limits of what sentence the defendants may receive.
[105] Interview with the AUSA's office, Los Angeles, February 1999.

[106] Interview with the AUSA's office, New York, and INS New York, May 1999.
[107] Global Survival Network, "Crime and Servitude: An Expose of the Traffic in Women for Prostitution from the Newly Independent States," October 1997.

to conspiracy to alien smuggling. Their sentences ranged from 2½ years to 6½ years with one ringleader getting 15 years.[108]

Some prosecutors contend that they are using the legal tools at their disposal, but there are high standards of proof in current involuntary servitude prosecutions. Moreover, some prosecutors say that they enter plea agreements in order to avoid having the victims testify at trial against their traffickers out of concern for the trauma that would result from public testimony and cross-examination. While each case is different and the prosecutors may not always be able to prove all of the indictable offenses, the general perception is that these sentences do not appear to account for all the human rights and civil violations inflicted upon the victims. In many of the cases, traffickers and brothel owners end up being prosecuted for hiring illegal aliens, immigration fraud, and/or the Mann Act which have limited penalties as opposed to kidnapping, RICO charges, peonage[109], money laundering, and collection of extension of credit by extortion.

Additionally, the criminal provisions of the labor statues—the most likely alternatives to slavery prosecutions—are especially weak, making it tough to prosecute traffickers of women for slave labor. The Fair Labor Standards Act (FLSA) carries criminal penalties for willful violations; however, it is only a six-month maximum sentence. A person convicted of a FLSA violation can only get a sentence involving prison time on the second conviction, though this issue is under review. The criminal penalties for intentional violations of the Migrant and Seasonal Agricultural Worker Protection Act (MSPA) is a statutory maximum of one year for the first offense and three years for the second or more offense. There are also no sentencing guidelines, so judges often give probation. Many prosecutors are therefore reluctant to take on labor cases that do not rise to the level of involuntary servitude. Prosecutors also find it difficult to file suit against farm owners who use slave labor, because the owners claim they were unaware of any exploitation on behalf of their contractors.[110] It is therefore necessary not only to strengthen the current labor statutes but also to provide for a statutory tool to punish those who benefit or profit from the slavery.

These low penalties and the long, complicated, and resource-intensive nature of trafficking cases tend to make them unattractive to many assistant US attorneys. Some Justice Department interlocutors claim that trafficking cases require enormous amounts of paperwork, and federal attorneys are frustrated that the sentencing outcomes historically have not reflected the work involved or the full nature of the crimes. There is no uniformity of opinion, however, about the issue. Other Department of Justice interlocutors feel the penalties for trafficking in women are tough enough but that the government must work harder to seek longer sentences allowable under the sentencing guidelines. Still, other prosecutors are very concerned that increased penalties will result in less pleas, more trials, additional trauma for the victims, and fewer cases being prosecuted as prosecutors are engaged in trials. They contend that the sentencing guidelines[111] are what matters, rather than the statutory maximums, pointing out that conspiracy prosecutions under 18USC241 carry a potential life sentence. And, when multiple substantive counts are charged (as in most federal involuntary servitude prosecutions), the statutory maximums for each count

---

[108] Sentencing hearing, US v. Cadena, West Palm Beach, Florida, April 16, 1999.
[109] Peonage is defined by case law as involuntary servitude for the purpose of repayment of a debt.

[110] Interview with Department of Justice, Civil Rights Division, Criminal Section, April 1999.
[111] The sentencing guidelines apply various factors to determine the actual sentence imposed within the statutory maximum.

aggregate to determine the full exposure, thus resulting in as much potential prison time as necessary to ensure a substantial sentence.

In 1996, Congress, concerned that the sentence guidelines did not adequately address the problem, directed the US Sentencing Commission to revise the guidelines for involuntary servitude and alien smuggling. These revisions raised the involuntary servitude guidelines to place them on par with kidnapping and extortion, and provided for enhancements in immigration cases where the aliens are injured or hurt.

Lack of a Trafficking Law

The US currently does not have a comprehensive trafficking law. Law enforcement now relies upon a number of criminal, labor, and immigration laws to address activities involved in trafficking schemes. Trafficking in women cases are may be prosecuted under various Title 18 sections, such as the Mann Act (§2421), involuntary servitude and slavery (§1581), and extortionate collection of extension of credit (§894). Cases are also prosecuted under Title 8 sections, such as recruiting, smuggling, and transporting aliens (§1324) or harboring for prostitution (§1328). Prosecutors feel the use of a combination of charges can create many plea and sentencing options to reward cooperation and/or reflect a defendant's role in the conspiracy as well as result in longer sentences. Moreover, currently there are a number of federal initiatives designed to address gaps in the laws regarding trafficking issues.

Advocates for a specific trafficking law, however, argue that using numerous statues may be more cumbersome as the prosecutor is required to prove each element of each crime whereas a trafficking statue would streamline

the prosecutorial burden. The passage of a trafficking law provides an additional tool without losing the existing mechanisms. Moreover, a trafficking law would permit better tracking of cases and record keeping, improve Department of Justice coordination, and serve as a greater deterrent to such behavior. Additionally, it would provide conceptual clarity, define the issue, and provide a model for other countries and for state and local legislation. Lastly, a trafficking law would also provide adequate protection and assistance for the trafficking victims.[112]

Law Enforcement May Miss "Mom and Pop" or Smaller Trafficking Cases

Many smaller trafficking in women situations may go unnoticed by US law enforcement. According to an Assistant US Attorney from New York, federal law enforcement tends to focus on major organized crime syndicates and may miss the smaller trafficking rings or "mom and pop" shop operations which commonly orchestrate trafficking in women operations. An INS agent in Los Angeles claims that there is more funding when cases involve organized crime, and that the smaller trafficking conspiracy cases therefore do not get as much attention and resources.

Local law enforcement may also miss possible trafficking instances. Local police officers tend not to be very interested in investigating brothels which is where much of the trafficking is occurring. Prostitution is sometimes seen as a victimless crime and therefore of lower priority than gang warfare, narcotics trafficking, or other street crimes. Victims' advocates claim that law enforcement often views trafficking victims as part of the conspiracy and consequently sees them as accomplices.

---

[112] Interviews with the President's Interagency Council on Women, September 1998-September 1999.

INS Challenges and Constraints

Some INS agents who have worked on trafficking cases say one of their largest challenges is that the victims are in the US illegally and thus must be treated the same as other undocumented workers because they have broken the law. Moreover, some INS agents say they need to be careful not to prejudice witnesses by promising them a green card or residency. Another primary challenge in their view is that they arrest over a million people a year and it is tough to determine who has been severely victimized or trafficked. According to one INS agent, it is hard to "play favorites" because there are countless other illegal aliens who are exploited by unscrupulous employers, and it is not easy to know where you draw the line in terms of who is being exploited. Some INS agents also believe that many of these cases are alien smuggling for prostitution cases not trafficking in women cases.

Even before the trafficking victims reach the border, State Department consular officers concede that mistakes are made in the visa process given the heavy volume of visa applicants. For example, there were approximately 98,000 visa applications in Bangkok in 1995.[113] And it is often the junior, less experienced foreign service officers who are conducting the visa interview. As consular officials try to be service-oriented and not "blanket deny" all young women between the ages of 15 and 30, potential trafficking victims may be missed.

Once at the border, some INS interlocutors claim it is difficult to be service-oriented, process people very rapidly at the border, and catch all potential trafficking victims. Resource issues often limit what INS can do. For example, INS has no means for tracking B2 (tourist) visa overstays, nor does it have an adequate means of checking into the schools that sponsor student visa applications. In New York, for example, there is only one person examining fraud cases involving invitations from schools.[114] Furthermore, according to an INS officer serving in Manila, INS is not committing any resources towards investigating marriage fraud. Though mail order bride companies from the Philippines and the US do not appear to be masking trafficking operations, with virtually no investigation, illegal trafficking situations could be missed.

INS agents also claim that they have a hard time getting law enforcement interested in their investigations involving minors, because some prosecutors believe most children have been smuggled into the country for family reunification and do not want to lock up or detain aliens who are minors. INS agents also say it is difficult to gain the trust of the children who have been convinced by the traffickers that INS wants to hurt them.

INS has also come under criticism for previous trafficking in women investigations. According to one California INS agent, mistakes, mismanagement, and neglect occurred in investigating the El Monte Thai slave labor case, resulting in the workers spending more time in slave-like conditions. In 1988, a notice of inspection for the El Monte compound was given to the perpetrators, the Manasurangkun family, three days in advance of the inspection. This gave the family time to scatter the workers. INS watched the workers scatter, but was helpless to do anything because the notice of inspection was an administrative, not criminal, action. Next, INS got an administrative subpoena that the family did not comply with. INS subsequently arrested the family for harboring aliens, but had to let them go for lack of evidence. INS then closed the case, claiming that the garment company was no longer in existence.

---

[113] Interview with the Consular Section, American Embassy in Bangkok, February 1999.

[114] Interview with INS, New York, December 1998.

INS got another investigative lead in 1992 to check out the compound, according to this INS agent. The Assistant US Attorney at the time required that INS meet a "shopping list" of things in order to establish probable cause and receive a search warrant. INS fulfilled the list, but not before the AUSA had changed and there were new requirements to meet. INS did not attempt to go after the additional requirements. A raid did not occur until August 1995 and it was conducted by the Department of Labor Standards Enforcement, who went in to cite the owners for doing industrial homework in a residential area, though INS assisted. This same INS agent, however, says that since the El Monte case, there has been a growing awareness by INS and other law enforcement entities that slavery actually exists in America. Subsequently, INS has taken the lead in pursuing several slavery cases, especially in the Los Angeles and Miami areas. INS was also commended recently for their assistance in a trafficking case in Chicago.

Intentionally Left Blank

XII. Issues and Challenges Associated with Providing Assistance to and Protecting Trafficking Victims

In addition to the challenges in investigating and prosecuting trafficking in women cases, non-governmental organizations (NGOs) claim there are numerous issues that make protecting trafficking victims difficult. Most of these issues center around the treatment of trafficking in women and children as an immigration issue focused on their illegal status, as opposed to a human rights issue. Additionally, there does not appear to be any consistency or streamlined procedures for housing and handling trafficking victims. The response often appears ad hoc and at the discretion of the local prosecutor, vice squad, FBI, or INS officials. Even the Attorney General herself has said that the government must do a better job of advocating for trafficking victims because right now there are not adequate protections for the victims.[115]

Detention and Deportation

Non-governmental organizations call for arrested trafficking victims to be housed in appropriate shelters, not in jail or detention facilities. Currently, they say that many trafficking victims are placed in INS detention facilities and then deported. Those few trafficking victims, who are designated material witnesses in federal criminal cases brought against the traffickers, may be placed in the US marshals' custody and held in local jails. Even when aliens are not being used as material witnesses, INS is housing over 60 percent of its detainees in local jails throughout the country, according to a 1998 report from Human Rights Watch. These INS detainees, including asylum seekers, are being held in jails where they might be mixed with accused and convicted criminal inmates. Human Rights Watch also reports that INS has not provided adequate oversight of its detainees inside these jails.[116]

It is impossible to determine how many trafficking victims are in detention centers; however, regular detention facilities, major contract facilities, and local jails housed over 150,000 aliens last year for an average of 32 days, according to INS's Director of Detention and Deportation. For juvenile aliens, the average length of stay in 1998 was 34 days, though the median was 12 days.[117] According to the US Director of the Jesuit Refugee Service, this detention has a negative consequence by criminalizing the victim in the mind of the public and fueling xenophobia. For trafficking victims, it also exacerbates all kinds of social, psychological, and medical problems. Additionally some lawyers, who specialize in assisting immigrant women say that they only learned about women who had been trafficked by chance through newspaper accounts of brothel raids, and that these women had not received proper medical attention while in detention.

- In a Florida case involving Mexican women and girls forced into prostitution, the victims spent time in both Krome, an INS detention center, and County Stockade, the local jail. In addition to Krome and Stockade, the minor victims were held in a juvenile detention center and a hotel where they were guarded 24 hours a day by INS. After three months, the victims went to a shelter found by their attorneys and paid through the government's Emergency Witness Assistance Program.[118]

Many INS agents concur that there needs to be more facilities for housing adult and minor trafficking victims, but say it does its best to treat trafficking victims humanely and make appropriate arrangements for them. This treatment is even more important for juvenile victims. While we do not know how many juvenile victims are being detained, the INS Juvenile Coordinator says INS houses about

---

[115] Interview with Attorney General Janet Reno, September 1999.
[116] Human Rights Watch United States, "Locked Away: Immigration Detainees in Jails in the United States," September 1998.

[117] Telephone interview with INS, Juvenile Coordinator, August 1999.
[118] Interview with FBI, INS agents, West Palm Beach, Florida, and Department of Justice, Civil Rights Division, Criminal Section, April 1999.

500 juvenile aliens a day in roughly 50 juvenile detention centers, group homes, shelter care facilities, and foster homes. Moreover, he says that the children receive education and medical care, and the staff and caseworkers at the facilities receive substantial training. At the same time, he concedes that more staff is needed, as juvenile aliens require additional resources and special attention. Some INS agents feel, however, that many US Attorneys are less inclined to take trafficking cases involving minors because of the lack of adequate facilities to hold them. In New York, for example, trafficking victims and aliens, who are minors, may end up in Spotford, a facility in Pennsylvania that houses criminal juveniles. This facility is also two hours from New York, making interactions with the victim witnesses difficult.[119] According to an INS agent in New York, INS is also out of witness fund money this year and does not dedicate money to sustain witnesses in temporary housing.

Trafficking victims, adults and minors who are not material witnesses are usually detained and then deported or voluntarily returned to their home country. Some victims are returned to their home countries after a videotaped deposition under Federal Rule of Criminal Procedure 15, which provides for the taking of pretrial testimony. In a recent example of deportation, Asian women, trafficked to the US for prostitution and forced to live in bondage until their contracts were paid off, were all deported immediately even before the case went to court or before they were able to recover any compensation or damages.

Victims' social service providers also worry about the lack of follow-through with deported trafficking victims, particularly given the involvement of crime groups in the trafficking industry and the potential for retaliation by these groups. According to a professor from California State University with an expertise in Southeast Asia and women's studies, some

non-profit organizations in Los Angeles are trying to partner up with NGOs abroad so that returnees can be met at the border or airport upon their return and receive repatriation assistance. In her opinion, these networks are easy to create but time consuming.

Lack of Adequate Shelters or Services for Trafficking Victims

At present, there are no shelters and precious little special funds specifically designed for trafficking victims. The existing shelters for domestic violence victims are the only current resources available for trafficking victims. Even these shelters may not always be available to trafficking victims as many shelters face funding constraints, and their limited program funds are frequently tied towards assisting a specific block or category of people, such as juveniles or rape victims.

Victims' advocates claim that on one level, most victims have basic needs such as shelter, medical, psychological, and/or legal services. There are, however, some unique considerations when it comes to trafficking victims. Attorneys for trafficking victims feel it is better for them to be housed together rather than split among several shelters. Trafficking victims have often bonded with one another because of their shared traumatic experiences. Many shelters, however, cannot accommodate a large influx of victims at once.

Furthermore, trafficking victims also have commonly experienced the most extreme forms of exploitation ranging from forced prostitution, involuntary confinement, rape, and torture. Thus, the need for mental health services is often greater than the counseling needs facing other victims.[120] In the Bowery brothel case, for example, one of the victims went crazy after years of confinement.[121]

---

[119] Interview with INS agents, New York, December 1998.

[120] Interview with the Little Tokyo Service Center, Coalition to Abolish Slavery and Trafficking, July 1999.

Trafficking victims may also speak a variety of foreign languages that shelters cannot accommodate. This contrasts with many domestic violence or rape victims who are American citizens or have been in the United States for a long time and speak English or Spanish. Additionally, trafficking victims often face complicated legal issues related to their immigration status. Shelters are not suppose to ask the immigration status of the women needing services, but some NGOs report that shelters are doing so. Shelters and clinics are permitted to give services to undocumented workers, but not direct compensation. The Legal Services Corporation (LSC),[122] provides funds to independent legal entities, but grantees are prohibited from representing illegal aliens in civil cases and grantees are not permitted to do criminal cases. There are a few limited exceptions that permit LSC recipients to use funds, from sources other than the Corporation, to assist illegal aliens or their children who suffer domestic violence;[123] however, this exception does not currently apply to illegal aliens who have suffered from trafficking.

Some existing shelters also express concern that trafficking victims pose greater security risks to the shelter given the trafficking industry's association with organized crime, crime rings, and gangs.[124] In several of the trafficking cases, victims who escaped from the brothels were hunted down by the traffickers and forcibly returned.

NGOs advocate that given these additional considerations and concerns, trafficking victims would be best served in either special shelters designed to meet their needs and/or existing shelters where the staff has been trained and given information on how to handle trafficking cases.

Difficulties with the "S" Visa

Non-governmental organizations claim that the use of the "S" visa, where the victim must possess critical and reliable information that is essential to a criminal case, is used too infrequently. NGOs claim, and many INS and law enforcement officers concur, that the "S" visa is not sufficient because there are only 200 "S" visas permitted a year, with an additional 50 available for those immigrants which possess significant information tied to terrorist actions. Many trafficking cases involve civil rather than criminal violations, yet the "S" visa can only be used in criminal cases. Law enforcement officers also lament the "S" visa's heavy oversight burden: the agents must closely supervise the "S" visa recipients and make quarterly reports to the Attorney General.[125] For example, the INS agent handling the El Monte Thai victims claims he has filed at least 700 forms relating to the "S" visa for the 75 victims. Every three months, he says, he must interview all of the victims to file the reports.[126] Some INS agents have expressed frustration that there is no "middle-road" between the "S" visa and straight deportation. Victims are sometimes given deferred action for a year, but this is a temporary measure.

In essence, many trafficking victims remain in a sort of legal limbo. Trafficking victims, who are waiting to be material witnesses at a trial,

---

[121] Interview with the AUSA's office, New York, May 1999.
[122] The Legal Services Corporation is an independent agency that receives funding from Congress. It was established by the Congressional Legal Services Corporation Act of 1974.
[123] Since 1998, an LSC grantee may use funds, derived from a source other than the Corporation, to provide legal assistance only to aliens, or their children, who have been battered or subjected to extreme cruelty in the United States by a spouse or a parent, or by a member of the spouse or parent's family residing in the same household as the alien. They may not use LSC funds for these purposes.
[124] Interview with the Coalition to Abolish Slavery and Trafficking, July 1999.

---

[125] INS Office of Policy and Planning, address before the US/Italy Bilateral Working Group on Trafficking in Women, July 1999.
[126] Interview, INS, Los Angeles, September 7, 1999.

also face economic hardships, as they are usually not permitted to work. Work authorization during this time period usually depends upon the discretion of the INS case agent. If the victim has been "paroled-in," there tends to be more latitude than if the victim has been given deferred status. To "parole-in"[127] an alien is also advantageous, as it limits the amount of "bad time" which would otherwise accrue, but it requires a letter from a senior Justice official.

In an effort to respond to these issues and provide visas to other aliens suffering serious abuses, the Department of Justice has proposed a new visa, called the "T" visa, in the upcoming crime bill. Aliens who have suffered severe physical or mental abuse in the US as a result of criminal activity will be eligible to obtain the "T" visa if they possess material information, not necessarily critical information, to the case. There will be 1,000 "T" visas a year for these victims and their family members. These visas also provide for work authorization. Lastly, the "T" visa will be valid for up to three years, and can be adjusted to permanent legal status for humanitarian reasons if necessary. Once the aliens became permanent residents, there would be offsets against the annual number permitted for a country.[128] Such a visa would not only be beneficial to law enforcement as it would ensure that they had material witnesses for their cases, but also would provide a "resting period" for the victims allowing them to receive some assistance.

---

[127] One option for legalizing a trafficking victim's immigration status is to bring the person into the US as a parolee in the public interest, which enables them to obtain work authorization but unfortunately often requires that the individual depart and re-enter the US for bureaucratic purposes. Another option, for those who have already been put in deportation proceedings, is suspension of deportation, which also can lead to work authorization but has the unfortunate side effect of the alien victim accruing "bad time" under Immigration Laws. "Bad time" affects the alien's chances of future legal entry.

---

[128] INS Office of Policy and Planning, address before the US/Italy Bilateral Working Group on Trafficking in Women, July 1999.

XIII. Calls For Change

The challenges associated with combating trafficking and protecting the victims are overwhelming but not unmanageable. The same government officials and non-governmental experts who outlined their most pressing issues also provided some suggestions and recommendations for preventing trafficking, prosecuting the traffickers, and assisting the trafficking victims. The Non-Governmental Organizations (NGOs) feel that a multi-dimensional approach to addressing and eradicating trafficking must include not only legislative initiatives, crime prevention, and border control efforts, but also social welfare, job training, rights protection, and development initiatives in the source, transit, and destination countries and locales. Developing effective strategies must entail governments, governmental agencies, NGOs, advocacy groups, service providers, survivors, and affected communities all working together on the issue.[129]

Prevention of Trafficking

Prevention of trafficking must incorporate economic alternatives in the source countries, public awareness campaigns, and improved data collection on the issue. Trafficking prevention strategies must focus on the high-risk areas in the primary source countries. Prevention initiatives should develop or expand upon targeted micro-credit initiatives, small business development, and job and skills training. Moreover, grants should be awarded to non-governmental organizations to promote or accelerate the empowerment of women in political, economic, social, and educational roles at the local, regional, and national levels in the source countries. Prevention of trafficking should also include legal, social, and cultural reforms to eliminate gender

discrimination. In a recent survey completed by 3,000 people in 57 regions of the Russian Federation and in Georgia, Armenia, Azerbaijan, Ukraine, and Mongolia, young and old women listed poverty, economic depression, and unequal career opportunities as their top three issues of concern.[130] High unemployment rates pose hardships on women. By some studies, between 70 and 80 percent of the unemployed workers in the Russian Federation, for example, are women.[131] For those women who have jobs, they often must contend with sexual harassment in the workplace. It is this destitution and discrimination that make women especially vulnerable to traffickers' false promises of good jobs abroad. In addition to addressing economic issues, NGOs call for programs to keep children, particularly girls, in elementary and secondary school as well as curricula which includes information about the dangers of trafficking. Some non-profit organizations claim that use of local drama clubs, student organizations, and church groups are not only cost effective but also a meaningful way to communicate with young people.

Additionally, NGOs say public awareness campaigns must involve the use of the media, particularly television, radio, newspapers, and magazines. In the survey mentioned above, television was clearly ranked first as the best way to reach at-risk young women and their families. Of those respondents who had heard of trafficking, 7 out of 10 people had learned about trafficking from TV. When asked about computer access, only 15 percent of the vulnerable 10 to 19-year-old population said they owned computers; however, 93 percent expressed a strong desire to use e-mail and the Internet.[132] While the insights learned from

[129] Miller, Ali and Stewart, Alison, International Human Rights Law Group, Report from the Roundtable on the Meaning of Trafficking in Persons: A Human Rights Perspective, Women's Rights Law Reporter, Rutger's Law School, Fall/Winter 1998.

[130] Puchkov, Yuri, Dr., "Report June 29, 1999 MiraMed Institute Anti-Trafficking Chatroom," MiraMed, June 29, 1999.
[131] USAID Office of Women in Development, Gender Matters Quarterly, "Women as Chattel: The Emerging Global Market in Trafficking, February 1999.

this survey in the Newly Independent States are very helpful, public awareness programs in other parts of the world must be culturally sensitive and focus on the most effective communication channels for that region. For example, skits and plays about the dangers of trafficking may be a better teaching tool in parts of Asia or elsewhere.

Thus, prevention of trafficking requires a better understanding of the individual source countries, traffickers, and their attempts to recruit girls from these nations. Additional information into the legal, economic, social, and cultural status of women in the individual source countries will also assist in developing prevention strategies. Strengthening the collection of trafficking data and research will be key to raising this level of comprehension. Some government experts who have studied the trafficking issue would like the Attorney General to establish guidelines for collecting data from federal, state, and local law enforcement agencies on human trafficking, particularly women and children, and the disposition of victims of these crimes. Data collected should be incorporated into existing and supplemental Department of Justice reports, including reports on criminal civil rights violations, organized crime, and exploitation of minors. The US is exploring additional ways to facilitate data-sharing, as appropriate, with law enforcement entities abroad, including developing further protocols.

Protection and Assistance for Trafficking Victims

There is a need for trafficking victims to receive medical, mental health, and legal services. Trafficking victims should have access to information about their rights and translation services. As mentioned earlier, appropriate shelters need to be constructed or designated for trafficking victims. Another solution is to

further utilize existing shelters as well as health and legal clinics in immigrant communities. Such shelters and clinics should be vetted beforehand to ensure they are capable of meeting the needs of trafficked victims. Moreover, staff at these shelters should receive specialized training. Government grants should also be awarded to those shelters and clinics with a proven track record of service, to enable them to provide victims with housing, medical, psychological, and legal services. In the area of legal services, the Legal Services Corporation Act might also be amended to permit LSC grantees to provide trafficking victims with legal services, similar to the exception that is made for illegal aliens who have subjected to domestic violence.

At present, the Department of Justice's Office for Victims of Crime and the victim-witness coordinators from the US Attorney's offices have the primary responsibility for ensuring the safety and protection of victims. The Office for Victims of Crime, Federal Crime Victims Division funds state compensation and state victim assistance programs. The Crime Victims Fund, established by the Victims Crime Act of 1984 and distributed to the states, is available to trafficking victims in terms of services but not in terms of direct funding. No state is permitted to give direct compensation to an undocumented worker only services.[133] Some government experts on the issue of trafficking would like trafficking victims in the US to be eligible for victim's services, compensation, and assistance under the Crime Victims Fund. Alternatively, a separate account, called the Trafficking Victims Protection Fund, might be established to provide the shelter and services for the trafficking victims. Criminal fines, penalties, and forfeited assets from the traffickers, which are not dispersed directly by the court to the trafficking victims, would go into this account.

[132] Puchkov, MiraMed Report, June 29, 1999.

[133] Department of Justice, Office for Victims of Crime, Federal Crime Victims Division, October 1999.

Additionally, some policymakers engaged on the issue would like funding from the Violence Against Women Act to be available to trafficking victims as well as for the operation of hotlines, training programs for professionals, and preparation of anti-trafficking informational materials.[134] Currently, funding from the Violence Against Women Act is for victims of domestic violence, stalking, and sexual assault.

Lastly, some NGOs call for better reintegration initiatives. In those cases where the trafficking victims will be returning home, advocates say an NGO representative should meet those victims at the border and/or airport. Well-thought out repatriation and reintegration programs should be in place to assist the trafficking victims make the transition and protect them from any retaliation by the traffickers.

Prosecution of Traffickers

To facilitate the investigation and prosecution of the traffickers, one Department of Justice civil attorney suggests that the Attorney General create trafficking and exploitation task forces in the United States Attorneys offices in districts with the highest number of trafficking and exploitation incidents.[135] This would be similar to organized crime and drug task forces. This approach differs from the current regional worker exploitation task forces, because it ensures that each US Attorney's office has permanent staff dedicated to these types of cases. These task forces would be beneficial, as they would ensure a higher profile, adequate staffing, and expertise. Currently, the US Attorneys offices appear to be understaffed and overburdened, making

investigations of potential trafficking cases difficult. Moreover, at present, many US Attorneys do not have a sufficient number of victim witness coordinators capable of working effectively with the victims. These task forces could be staffed by Assistant US Attorneys and detailees from DOJ's Criminal Division and/or the Civil Rights Division's Criminal Section.

To improve coordination and information-sharing, these task forces should work with local law enforcement, including the local district attorney and chief of police. This would also assist in the proper labeling of cases, since many trafficking or exploitation cases are frequently labeled as straight alien smuggling or prostitution cases. Additional recommendations include monthly meetings with the US Attorneys, the local police, the District Attorney's Office, INS, and FBI as well as tapping into NGO expertise and experience with trafficking victims.[136]

Advocates for trafficking victims also believe that federal, state, and local law enforcement, including immigration officials, should receive specialized training in identifying and responding to trafficking victims. This training should also include sensitized questions to be used in debriefing the victims. In an effort to bolster training, INS, with the assistance of the Office for Victims of Crime, has put together an informational training video to help sensitize the INS and border patrol agents to victims needs. The Attorney General has said that it is absolutely critical to educate state and local agencies as they are the "eyes and ears" in these regions as well as for local, state, and federal law enforcement to work collaboratively on this issue.[137] Training for State Department consular officers and diplomatic security agents should also be bolstered. Additional instruction should be

[134] Interviews with the President's Interagency Council on Women.
[135] Interview with an attorney at the Department of Justice, Civil Rights Division, Office of the Special Counsel for Immigration Related Unfair Employment Practices, March 1999.

[136] Interview with an attorney at the Department of Justice, Civil Rights Division, Office of the Special Counsel for Immigration Related Unfair Employment Practices, March 1999.
[137] Interview with the Attorney General, September 1999.

given on identifying the "front companies" used by the traffickers and the range of auxiliary members involved in the trafficking operations, such as the recruiters, transporters, and document forgers.

Deterring, disrupting, and prosecuting traffickers will also require strengthening the laws and penalties against trafficking in women and/or drafting new trafficking legislation. Prosecutors practicing in this area would like involuntary servitude statutes to be modified to recognize psychological pressures, not just force and threats. Some experts in the trafficking field recommend that trafficking in women and children should carry sentences of 15 years or more. Moreover, they suggest that the US Sentencing Commission shall further review and, if appropriate, amend the sentencing guidelines applicable to persons convicted of offenses relating to trafficking, involuntary servitude, peonage, and slave trade offenses. The sentencing guidelines should be sufficiently stringent to reflect the heinous nature of such offenses. Sentencing enhancements should be considered when the offenses include a large number of victims, involve a pattern of continued and flagrant violations, include the use or threatened use of a weapon, and result in the death or bodily injury of any person. Other possible sentencing enhancements could include: bribery and graft in connection with trafficking, money laundering of profits, organized crime involvement, sexual assault, the trafficking of underage victims, and the transport of victims in an unsafe manner.

Under a new trafficking law and/or enhanced penalties, upon conviction for a trafficking violation, the convicted person should be required to forfeit any property traceable to gross profits or other proceeds obtained from such offenses or used to promote the commission of such transgressions.[138] Courts should also be directed to order the defendants to pay restitution to the victims in addition to any other civil or criminal penalties authorized by law. The forfeited property could be used to pay this restitution. NGOs also call for trafficked persons to be able to more easily file civil claims and for judgments against their traffickers. Judgments in those claims could be satisfied from the forfeited assets. Stiffer penalties for traffickers may also serve as a model for other countries that are crafting their anti-trafficking legislation.

Without implementation of these proposals, trafficking in women—this modern-day form of slavery in the United States—will not only continue but also will grow. Given the extensive profits of the industry and countless targets of opportunity, it is only a matter of time until the large organized criminal syndicates involved in trafficking overseas become more heavily involved in trafficking in the US. Thus, improving law enforcement coordination and information-sharing as well as strengthening the penalties for traffickers will be key to prosecuting those who traffic in women. At the same time, economic alternatives and effective prevention programs, including public awareness campaigns in the source countries, will arm the women with jobs and information making them less vulnerable to the traffickers. Lastly, providing shelter and services for trafficking victims will not only provide law enforcement with invaluable witnesses in their criminal cases against the traffickers, but also will exemplify the humanitarian ideals of respect and dignity for the individual on which US law is based.

---

[138] Interviews with the President's Interagency Council on Women.

APPENDIX I:
Matrix of Some of the Major Trafficking Cases[139] in the United States Over the Last Eight Years

Case Summaries

In the last three years, the Department of Justice has prosecuted numerous "modern-day slavery" and trafficking cases. The Department's Involuntary Servitude Coordinator alone has prosecuted slavery cases involving over 150 victims. These trafficking cases involved varying degrees of deception, confinement, force, and grievous human rights abuses. These cases were not specific to one region, having occurred around the country. These cases do not offer an exhaustive list of prosecutions, as they do not list state law enforcement efforts. They do provide, however, a glimpse into the civil rights violations and US government efforts to combat them.

US v. Cadena 1998
Background/Deception: From about February 1996 to about March 1998, some 25 to 40 Mexican women and girls, some as young as 14 years old, were trafficked from the Veracruz state in Mexico to Florida and the Carolinas in the United States. The victims had been promised jobs in waitressing, housekeeping, landscaping, childcare and elder care. Upon their arrival, the women and girls were told they must work as prostitutes in brothels serving migrant workers or risk harm to themselves and/or their families.

Confinement: Besides enduring threats, women who attempted to escape were subjugated to beatings. Guards used force to keep them in the brothels in order that they pay off their smuggling debt that ranged from $2,000 to $3,000. One woman was locked in a closet for 15 days as punishment for trying to escape. Additional human rights abuses included: forced prostitution, assault, rape, and forced abortions.

---

[139] The information on the major trafficking cases listed below comes from a variety of sources, most notably from the Department of Justice, Civil Rights Division, Criminal Section and INS headquarters. It is not an exhaustive list of the trafficking and slavery cases in the United States.

Outcome: In March 1998, 16 men were indicted in Florida for enslaving the Mexican women and girls in brothels. The men were charged with importing aliens for immoral purposes, transporting women and minors for prostitution, involuntary servitude, visa fraud, conspiracy, and violation of civil rights. The defendants' sentences ranged from 2 ½ to 6 ½ years, with one ringleader receiving 15 years. The judge ordered that the trafficking organization pay $1 million dollars in restitution. Several of the other key ringleaders had previously fled to Mexico. The United States is working with the Mexican government to secure their capture. The victims, who are currently living in Florida at either a shelter or on their own, did receive some money from the traffickers seized assets in the US.

US v. Mishulovich 1999
Background/Deception: From around October 1996 to August 1997, a Russian-American named Alexander Mishulovich was involved in large scale visa fraud, recruiting Latvian women in Riga to come to Chicago, Illinois to dance in bikinis in respectable, sophisticated nightclubs. The women were told that they would earn significant sums of money— $60,000 a year—and there would be no nudity. Mishulovich instructed the women to falsely represent their intentions when presenting themselves to the American Embassy. Upon arrival however, the women were forced to dance topless and nude. He took the women's passports and visas, which he offered to sell back to them for up to $60,000. Later on, he ultimately sold the passports back to some of the women for $4,000 in cash.

Confinement: The women were not permitted to return to Latvia without paying off their smuggling debt. The women were also locked in apartments or hotel rooms, routinely beaten, and maltreated to secure their continued cooperation. Mishulovich and his co-conspirators took through force and threats the money the young women earned from dancing. Mishulovich threatened to kill the young women and their family members through his extensive organized crime connections if the women failed to accede to his demands.

Outcome: On September 10, 1998 Mishulovich, another Russian, and two Latvians were arrested for a variety of offenses including peonage, conspiracy to commit offense or fraud, and obstructing law enforcement. The arrests also resulted in the recovery of 11 weapons, ammunition, documents, and photographs identifying additional victims. The case is scheduled to go to trial this December. Two to three of the victims returned home voluntarily while others are living in the US on their own while awaiting the trial.

US v. Kwon 1998
Background/Deception: From on or about June 1995 until on or about January 1998, defendants recruited and transported Chinese-Korean women from China to the Commonwealth of the Northern Mariana Islands for the purpose of exploiting and abusing them for profit. They were promised legitimate waitressing jobs but then forced to work at a karaoke club and submit to customer's sexual demands. Some of the women also complained of physical and sexual abuse by their bosses.

Confinement: The women were held at a barracks apartment. The defendants took their passports, visas, and airline tickets. The women were only allowed to leave the barracks apartment with permission and an escort. The women were threatened with violence, including death, if they left or attempted to leave without paying their debt.

Outcome: Three defendants were indicted on November 1998 for conspiracy against rights, involuntary servitude, extortion, transportation for illegal sexual activity, and the use of a firearm in the commission of a crime of violence. They pled guilty to conspiracy to violate the 13th Amendment and laws governing involuntary servitude, extortion, and transportation for illegal sexual purposes. Their sentences will likely range from 2 to 8 years. The victims are currently living on their own in apartments in Guam working at jobs the Department of Justice helped them acquire.

US v. Milan Lejhanec and Ladislav Ruc 1998
Background/Deception: The defendants placed advertisements in a Czech newspaper soliciting women to work in legitimate jobs in the United States. Upon arrival in the US the women found out the legitimate jobs did not exist, and they were forced to work in New York City strip clubs where customers fondled them for a fee.

Confinement: The women's passports were taken and they were not free to leave until they had paid off their smuggling debt.

Outcome: Both defendants received sentences of approximately five years incarceration for trafficking women into the US for prostitution or other immoral purposes, with two additional defendants being charged with witness tampering.

US v. Zheng Qiaochhai, Zheng Qioyu, and Lin Xiao 1998
Background/Deception: The defendants recruited women in China for jobs as waitresses in the Commonwealth of the Northern Marianas Islands in the District of Guam. Shortly after the women arrived and started working in the bar, they were pressed into service as prostitutes.

Outcome: The defendants were convicted of two counts of conspiracy and transporting women in foreign commerce for purposes of prostitution by a jury in Saipan.

US v. Paoletti 1997

Background/Deception: Since the early 1990s, the Paoletti family is believed to have trafficked over 1,000 deaf and mute Mexican women and men. The Mexicans were brought to the United States believing they would have good jobs. Once they arrived, they were forced to hawk trinkets and beg on subways and buses. They had a daily quota, and were beaten or mistreated if they did not make their quota.

Confinement: They were held under slave-like conditions, and not allowed to return to Mexico. The Paolettis held their documents under lock and key. Those who tried to leave were hunted down and returned to the workhouses. They were punished with beatings, forced menial labor, and constant supervision. In a few instances, stun guns were used on the victims as a form of punishment.

Outcome: Some 70 deaf Mexicans were found during a raid. In New York, a total of 20 persons were indicted on charges of: aiding and abetting; conspiracy; the bringing in, transporting, harboring, and inducement to enter of illegal aliens; the interference of commerce by threats or violence; and involuntary servitude. Eighteen pled guilty to their respective indictments. Adriana Lemus, the ringleader, received 14 years in prison, with the other co-conspirators receiving 1-to-8 year sentences depending on their involvement in the criminal scheme. In Charlotte, two defendants in the case pled guilty to aiding and abetting; conspiracy; and the bringing in, transporting, harboring and inducement to enter of illegal aliens. One defendant received a prison term of almost four years, the other received three years and four months. It is estimated that the Paoletti family made some $8 million dollars before they were arrested, and the judge ordered $1 million dollars in restitution in October 1998.

US v. Wattanasiri 1995

Background/Deception: In conjunction with Thai traffickers, Ludwig Janak, a German national who operated a tour guide service in Thailand, recruited Thai women to come to the United States to work. Several of the women were told they would have good jobs working in restaurants. Once in the US, Thai traffickers and a Korean madam forced the women into prostitution.

Confinement: The women were held against their will at a brothel house and forced to work as prostitutes until their $35,000 smuggling debt was paid off. The women were kept in the underground brothel by bars on the windows and 24-hour surveillance. The defendants required that each woman sleep with four to five hundred customers to pay off the smuggling fee.

Outcome: A total of 18 defendants were indicted on charges of kidnapping, alien smuggling, extortion, and white slavery. Twelve defendants were successfully prosecuted; the rest had fled to Thailand. Thus far, only two have been extradited from Thailand. The defendants were given sentences of between four and nine years.

US v. Manasurangkun 1995

Background/Deception: Some 70 to 78 Thai laborers, predominantly women from impoverished backgrounds with little education, were brought to the United States. The Thai traffickers promised the women high wages, good working hours, and freedom. Once they arrived in the United States, they were forced to labor in a sweatshop, working some 20-hour shifts in a garment factory.

Confinement: These Thai nationals were held against their will and systematically abused. The laborers were incarcerated in primitive conditions in a clandestine garment factory.

High perimeter walls, razor wire, and corrugated steel panels were erected to conceal the facility. Additionally, around the clock sentries were installed to ensure no one escaped from the compound. The workers were made to pay an indentured servitude debt of between $8,000 and $15,000 and forced to write fake letters home, praising their working conditions.

Outcome: Seven defendants were convicted of alien smuggling, involuntary servitude, and civil rights violations. They received sentences ranging from four to seven years, with one defendant receiving seven months. Restitution in the amount of $4.5 million was ordered for the victims. Two additional defendants remain fugitives.

Why Women Are Trafficked to the United States*

Prostitution	Latin America: (Mexican victims) US v. Cadena 1998
	Asia: (Chinese-Korean victims) US v. Kwon 1998
	Asia: (Korean, Mexican, and Thai victims) US v. Kim, Phan, and Ortiz 1998
	Asia: (Chinese victims) US v. Zheng Qiaochhai, Zheng Qioyu, Lin Xiao 1998
	Asia: (Chinese victim) US v. Can 1997
	Asia: (Thai victims) US v. Wattanasiri 1995
	Asia: (Thai, Malaysian, and Singaporean victims) Operation Ling 1997
Stripping/ Sexual Touching	NIS: (Latvian victims) US v. Mishulovich 1999
	Central Europe: (Czech Republic victims) US v. Lejhanec and Ruc 1998
Sweatshop Labor	Asia: (Chinese victims) AFL-CIO, Global Exchange, Sweatshop Watch, Union of Needletrades Industrial and Textile Employees, and Asian Law Caucus. v. The Gap, The Associated Merchandising Corp., Cutter and Buck, Inc, Dayton-Hudson Corp., The Dress Barn, The Gymboree Corp., J.C. Penney Company, J.Crew Group, Jones Apparel Group, Lady Bryant, The Limited, The May Department, Nordstrom, Oshkosh B'Gosh, Sears Roebuck and Company, Tommy Hilfiger, Wal-Mart, Warnaco Group, and Does 1-400 1999
	Asia: (Thai victims) US v. Manasurangkun 1995
Agricultural Slave Labor	Latin America: (Mexican victims) US v. Cuello 1999
	Latin America: (Mexican and Guatemalan victims) US v. Flores 1997
Domestic Servitude	India: (Indian victim) US v. Mahtani 1996
	Middle East: (Sri Lankan victim) US v. Alzanki 1995
	Latin America: (Mexican victim) US v. Vargas 1991
Other Servitude	Latin America: (Mexican victims) US v. Lozano 1998
	Latin America: (Mexican victims) US v. Paoletti 1997

*This is not an exhaustive list of all of the trafficking and slavery cases, but it does represent some of the more prominent and recent cases, and it exemplifies the various reasons why women are trafficked to the United States.

Characterization of the Traffickers in the United States

In the United States, trafficking in women and children is primarily being conducted by smaller crime rings and loosely connected criminal networks. The nucleus of several of these crime rings centers around a family. There may be additional overlaps among the categories as many crime rings use their connections abroad to contract out duties. It is this amorphous nature of these rings and networks that make combating trafficking in women a challenging problem for law enforcement.

Small crime ring:
US v. Mishulovich
US v. Ruc
US v. Cadena
Operation Ling

Family crime ring:
US v. Paoletti
US v. Lozano
US v. Can
US v. Mahtani
US v. Kwon

Loosely connected criminal network:
US v. Wattanasiri
US v. Manasurangkun
Project Orphan

Gangs:
- Hmong case, Fresno-based gang involved in internal trafficking in California.

- Flying Dragons, a Chinese street gang that has provided protection to brothels where trafficking is thought to have occurred. The Flying Dragons is considered the enforcement sector of the HipsingTriad, a Fukienese Triad.

- Black Dragons and Koolboyz, Asian street gangs that have provided protection to brothels where trafficking is also thought to have occurred.

Note: The following Asian criminal organizations—the Sun Yee On Triad, 14K Triad, Wo Hop To Triad, the United Bamboo Gang, and Fuk Ching Gang—are involved in alien smuggling to the United States and it is likely that their activities include trafficking.

The following major Russian organized crime syndicates—the Izmailovskaya, Dagestantsy, Kazanskaya, and Solntsenskaya—are involved in the prostitution industry throughout the United States. Given the way these organized crime syndicates operate overseas and the brutality of these organizations, it is likely that this involvement in the US includes trafficking in women through the use of deception, threats, and violence.

General Time Span of the Trafficking Operations

A review of trafficking and slavery operations, involving sweatshop, agricultural, and other forms of labor, over the last eight years showed that these operations went unnoticed or were able to exist longer than sex trafficking operations. Labor trafficking operations generally lasted from 4½ to 6½ years, whereas trafficking operations for prostitution lasted from a little over a year to approximately 2½ years before being discovered. Trafficking operations for other forms of the sex industry, such as exotic dancing and peep and touch shows, were in existence for anywhere from ten months to three years. Once uncovered, trafficking and slavery cases usually take about a year and a half to investigate and prosecute, according to the Department of Justice's Involuntary Servitude Coordinator in the Civil Rights Division, Criminal Section.

- US v. Wattanasiri: January 1994 – March 1995 (1 year and about 3 months).

- US v. Can: Beginning on or about September 24, 1994 to about April 19, 1996 (1 year and 7 months or so).

- US v. Kwon: June 1995 to about January 1998 (2 years and 7 months).

- US v. Cadena: February 1996 to March 1998 (2 years and 1 month).

- US v. Mishulovich: October 1996 to about August 1997 (10 months).

- US v. Ruc: Mid-1995 to about July 6, 1998 (About three years).

- US v. Manasurangkun: From about April 1989 to about August 2, 1995 (6 years and 4 months).

- CNMI labor suit: 1993 to the present (6 years).

- US v. Flores: From the late 1980s to fall 1996 (over 6 years).

- US v. Mahtani: Early 1995 to February 8, 1996 (roughly 1 year, 1 month).

- US v. Paoletti: From approximately January 1993 to about July 1997 (4 years and 6 months).

- US v. Lozano: From about June 1992 to about 1998 (6 years).

Routes to and within the United States:
- US v. Wattanasiri: Bangkok to Bowery area of New York City, New York.
  Staging areas: Connecticut, Brooklyn, and Chinatown. Women also sent to: San Francisco, Dallas, Charlotte, and Kentucky.

- US v. Can: PRC to Mexico to Washington, DC to New York to Los Angeles, California.

- US v. Kwon: PRC to Saipan, Commonwealth of the Northern Mariana Islands (CNMI).

- US v. Cadena: Veracruz state, Mexico to Houston, Texas to Florida. Once in Florida, the women and girls were rotated among brothels in the following Florida cities: Avon Park, Ft. Myers, Ft. Pierce, Haines City, Lake Worth, Okeechobee, Ocoee, Orlando, Tampa, and Zolfo Springs. They were also rotated between Lake City and John's Island in South Carolina.

- US v. Mishulovich: Riga, Latvia to Chicago, Illinois. Defendants also tried to recruit women in Minsk, Belarus.

- US v. Ruc: Prague, Czech Republic to Brooklyn and New York City, New York.

- US v. Manasurangkun: Bangkok, Thailand to Los Angeles, California to El Monte, California.

- US v. Paoletti: Mexico to California to Los Angeles to Queens, New York and Chicago, Illinois. The Mexican victims were also transported to Boston, Massachusetts, Washington, DC, Baltimore, Maryland, Los Angeles, California, and Philadelphia, Pennsylvania, Sanford, North Carolina.

- US v. Lozano: Mexico to El Paso, Texas and elsewhere in the US, including Albuquerque, New Mexico. The victims were transported among various cities including but not limited to Sanford, North Carolina, Los Angeles, California, Albuquerque, New Mexico, Tucson, Arizona, and Phoenix, Arizona.

- US v. Flores: Chandler Heights, Arizona at the US/Mexico border to Clarendon County, South Carolina.

- US v. Mahtani: Bombay, India to Florida.

- US v. Alzanki: Kuwait to Quincy, Massachusetts.

B1/B2 Visa Time Length from Major Source Countries for the US[140]

B1 (Business) B2 (Tourism)

Country:	Fee:
Russia:	Multiple-entry visa valid for up to 12 months $150
	Multiple-entry visa valid for up to 36 months $450
Ukraine:	One entry valid for up to 6 months $30
	Two entries valid for up to 6 months $60
	Multiple-entry valid for up to 36 months $120
Latvia:	Multiple-entry valid for up to 120 months no fee
The Czech Republic:	Multiple-entry valid for up to 120 months no fee
Poland:	Multiple-entry valid for up to 120 months no fee
Thailand:	Multiple-entry valid for up to for 120 months no fee
The Philippines:	Multiple-entry valid for up to 120 months no fee
China:	Multiple-entry valid for up to 6 months no fee
Mexico:	Multiple-entry valid for up to 120 months no fee

Note: Citizens wishing to travel to the United States from any of these countries—including those which say no fee—must pay an additional $45. This fee covers the costs associated with the machine readable visa equipment.

---

[140] Information from the Department of State, Bureau of Consular Affairs, Visa Office.

Intentionally Left Blank

APPENDIX II:
International Organized Crime and its Involvement in Trafficking Women and Children Abroad

A review of US embassy, press, and non-governmental reports show that international criminal organizations are much more heavily involved in trafficking in women and children overseas than they are in the United States. The international trafficking trade appears to be highly organized, involving sophisticated international networks of procurers, document forgers and providers, escorts, organizers, financiers, corrupt officials, and brothel operators. International organized crime has capitalized on weak economies, corruption, and improved international transportation infrastructure to traffic some 700,000 to two million women and children globally each year. Southeast Asia comprises nearly one-third of this global trade. The Newly Independent States and Eastern Europe have risen to roughly one-fourth of the world's trade, making it one of the faster growing regions in the world.[141] The number of organized crime groups engaged in trafficking is likely to continue increasing, given the high profit potential and relatively low penalties.

Asian Organized Crime

On April 23 1999, ministers from eighteen Asia-Pacific countries issued the Bangkok declaration stating that they are gravely concerned by the increasing activities of transnational organized criminal groups who are profiting from trafficking in human beings, especially women and children. They also said that the participating countries should be encouraged to pass legislation to criminalize trafficking in human beings, especially women and children, in all its forms and purposes, including as sources of cheap labor. They called for countries to cooperate as necessary

in the prosecution and penalization of all offenders, especially international organized criminal groups.[142]

Regional destination countries, such as Australia, have noticed a rise in women trafficked to their countries and the involvement of organized crime in the industry. Australia's Justice Minister stated last year that there had been a noticeable increase in the number of Asian women lured to Australia with the pretense of legitimate jobs only to find themselves working in virtual slavery in legal and illegal brothels. International crime syndicates, some with links to the drug trade, are arranging the women's movement.[143] The American consulate in Sydney reports that Southeast Asian women are being trafficked to Australia by international organized crime syndicates, such as the 14K, a Chinese triad. There is evidence of organized crime groups making multi-million-dollar profits from prostitution, much of it untaxed and moved offshore.

The Triads

Major Asian organized crime groups are involved in trafficking women and children. In China, the Sun Yee On, 14 K, Big Circle Boys, and Wo On Lok Triads have all repeatedly been linked to smuggling illegal immigrants and prostitution rackets. The American Embassy in London reports that Chinese Triads are the primary traffickers of women and girls from Southeast Asia, South America, and Eastern Europe to Britian. Press reports indicate that Chinese Triads have also worked with Russian organized crime groups in trafficking. Upon arrival, the victims are held prisoner until further money is paid or they are

---

[141] Central Intelligence Agency briefing, Global Trafficking in Women and Children: Assessing the Magnitude, April 1999.

[142] Cable from the American Embassy in Bangkok, 005518, April 23, 1999.
[143] "Australia to Crack Down on Asian Sex Slaves," Agence Fance Presse, April 14, 1998.

forced into bonded labor, such as sweatshops or prostitution.[144] Italian prosecutors maintain that Chinese, Albanian, and Nigerian crime groups dominate the trafficking and slave trade in Italy, with the Chinese largely involved in slave labor.[145] Thirty-three members of the Serpents Head—the Milan cell of the Grand Dragon Triad, were sentenced in Italy in September 1998 for trafficking.[146]

Malaysian police and non-governmental organizations believe that ethnic Chinese criminal syndicates are behind most of the trafficking in their country. Trafficked women are usually fed into an extensive system of Chinese owned lounges, nightclubs, and brothels that exist throughout much of Asia.[147]

Chinese criminal organizations have also been involved in abducting and selling women and children in China itself. For example, the Song clan group in Lixin county in Anhui set up special operations in Chengdu under the guise of hiring people to go to Shanghai to get apparel or go to Anhui to purchase traditional Chinese medicines. Lured under false pretenses, the young women were then kidnapped and delivered to buyers.[148]

The Yakuza

The American Embassy in Tokyo reports that Japanese organized crime or the Yakuza are involved in trafficking in women and the adult entertainment industry. Local brokers approach women in their home country and offer well-paying jobs in legitimate professions abroad. Once in Japan, they are funneled to their actual employers by intermediaries, primarily Japanese, who often have purchased the rights to these women from the source country brokers. The usual pay for these women is 2 million yen or approximately $14,000 to $15,000 at 1998 exchange rates.

According to a Wellesley College professor who is researching trafficking in women and traveled to Japan last spring, the Yakuza have increasingly become involved in the trafficking of persons since the bubble economy burst in 1992 and they had to look for additional means of income. She reports that the Yakuza view trafficking in women as a business and protect their "investment" by detailing a "bodyguard" to monitor the movements of each woman or girl. They will post pictures of a woman or girl who has escaped, and encourage members or affiliates to turn her in if found. This professor claims that corruption is a problem as the police are often the ones who turn the escapee in to the mob. The US Legal Attaché serving in Manila reports that those Filipinas who have tried to flee in Japan have been killed. Non-governmental organizations also claim that several shelters for escapees had been vandalized severely by the Yakuza in the last few years. Subsequently, the shelters changed locations and now operate under cover.

The Japanese National Police Agency concurs that there has been a rise in foreigners forced into prostitution in Japan. The women, mostly from Asia and Latin America, are commonly recruited to be bar hostesses, but on arrival are forced into prostitution. They are kept under constant surveillance and all earnings are turned over to the traffickers.[149] Investigations by the non-governmental organization Global Survival Network, reveal that the Japanese Yakuza are involved in the trafficking industry, often in cooperation with the Russian mafia. The Yakuza not only force Russian women,

[144] Bennetto, Jason, "Triads Target British Sex Trade," The Independent, August 11, 1997, Johnston, Philip, "Triads and Mafia Cash in on Illegal Immigrants," The Daily Telegraph, November 27, 1997.
[145] Discussions with the US-Italy Bilateral Working Group on Trafficking in Women, July 1999.
[146] Cable from the American Consulate in Milan 00828.
[147] Cable from the American Embassy in Kuala Lumpur 000950, April 21, 1999.
[148] "China: How Criminal Organizations Acquire Illicit Wealth," Daily Report China, August 12, 1997.

[149] "Japan Reports Rise in Foreigners Forced Into Prostitution," Agence France Presse, April 6, 1998.

who thought they were going to work in Japan as hostesses, into prostitution but also traffic Thai and Mexican women to Japanese brothels. The Thai women are frequently bought from Thai traffickers, while the Mexican women are duped into thinking they would be singers or actresses in Japan. The Yakuza have also been known to traffic women from the United States to Japan.[150]

The Yakuza also work with Filipino recruiters to traffic Filipina women to Hong Kong and Japan, according to the legal attaché in Manila. The Yakuza use local illegal recruiters to get the women to go to Japan to work as bar hostesses, but many are then forced into prostitution. Batis, a Manila non-governmental organization, agrees that the Yakuza are working with local recruiters in Manila. Batis reports that a variety of sex establishments are owned by the Yakuza in the Philippines and in Japan. Women are held in these clubs in Japan under the supervision of the Yakuza. A recruiter gets paid $6,000 to $10,000 per woman he recruits to go to Japan. The club then pays the recruiter. Batis claims that the recruiter often targets the most vulnerable women, who are usually from the typhoon areas.

Thai Criminal Networks

Besides the Triads and the Yakuza, Thai criminal networks are involved in trafficking in women. Law enforcement reports that there are at least seven "families" in Bangkok, Thailand who recruit, sell, and smuggle Asian women throughout the world, including the US, to serve as prostitutes. These families secure identity/travel documents, arrange travel itineraries, and then broker the women to agents representing brothels in the US, Japan, Canada, and Australia. The agents charge the

women roughly $40,000 to effect entry into the US. Upon entry, the agent is responsible for paying a fee to the smuggling organization in Thailand. The female's debt is repaid by her engagement in prostitution. Until the payment is made, the woman is under the control of the agent and is frequently sold, battered, or exchanged. The women are smuggled into a foreign country utilizing photo-substituted or impostor Thai passports. After arrival the passports are usually returned to the smuggler in Thailand and recycled. The Thai smugglers use escorts called "jockeys" to transport the females to the US. The jockey is paid $1,000 per person for the trip. He assists in getting the non-English speaking women through the INS and Customs inspection process. After clearing Customs, the jockey delivers the women to the domestic agent who will then place her with the brothel.

Russian Organized Crime

Russian organized crime's traditional involvement in prostitution has grown to include trafficking. Russian organized crime provides "the roof," or cover for trafficking operations, while lower-level Russian criminals manage recruitment and logistics. Russian criminals often operate behind the facades of employment, travel, modeling, and/or matchmaking agencies. The Global Survival Network concurs that traffickers use matchmaking or marriage agency databases to identify women looking for a better life abroad. Another American non-governmental organization, MiraMed, says traffickers in Russia have gone so far as to set up "career day" booths in institutes and universities, promising profitable work abroad. Traffickers often provide women with counterfeit travel documents or assist them in obtaining genuine documents through fraud. Russian organized crime groups are reportedly cooperating with Albanian, Turkish, former Yugoslavian crime

---

[150] Global Survival Network, "Crime and Servitude: An Exposé of the Traffic in Women for Prostitution from the Newly Independent States," October 1997.

groups, Chinese Triads, and the Japanese Yakuza to traffic women to Western Europe and Japan.[151]

The International Organization for Migration and the Global Survival Network report that Russian organized crime groups control European prostitution industries, such as those in Poland, Germany, and Italy. Bulgarian Interior Ministry Chief Secretary Bozhidar Popov has also said that Russian criminals are trafficking Russian, Ukrainian, Georgian, and Chechen women through Bulgaria to Turkey, Greece and elsewhere in Western Europe for prostitution. One major Russian criminal syndicate, the Mogilevich organization, owns night clubs in Prague, Riga, and Kiev and has engaged in trafficking in women for forced prostitution at these clubs.[152] The powerful Izmailovskaya syndicate is under intense investigation by a variety of European law enforcement structures for involvement in trafficking in women and children as well as drug trafficking and counterfeit cigarette manufacturing. Lithuanian Member of Parliament Vilija Aleknaite-Abramikiene reports that Russian organized crime groups are heavily involved in trafficking women for the sex industry in Lithuania. In Russia's Far East, Russian criminals reportedly supplied Russian women to brothels and clubs in Hong Kong and Macao.

Commander Ina Volf of the Israeli national police believes that Russian organized crime is involved in trafficking from the Newly Independent States.[153] A report by Israel's Women's Network found that Russian organized crime controls the sex industry throughout Israel. There are roughly nine to ten Russian prostitution rings operating in Israel. Territory has been divided among the crime bosses. It has become a whole industry; recruiting the women, bringing them to Israel, and distributing them to the various brothels.[154] Knesset member Marina Solodkin claims that local Israeli mafioso are also involved in the trafficking industry.[155]

Israel's Women's Network also reports that a protection racket has grown up around the trafficking and prostitution business in Israel. There is a symbiotic relationship between the police and pimps in which pimps may provide useful intelligence to police on criminal activity in Israel. The police see them as valuable sources of information and work to turn the pimps into collaborators. Overall, trafficking and prostitution is a lucrative business in Israel where Soviet-immigrant Israeli bosses make anywhere from $1,000 to $4,000 a day off the women.

Elsewhere in the Middle East, police and other sources in the United Arab Emirates generally believe that crime organizations from Russia and the Newly Independent States are involved in local prostitution involving women from their countries, according to the American Embassy in Dubai.

Besides Europe, Asia, and the Middle East, Russian organized crime is involved in trafficking women to Canada, according to the American Embassy in Toronto. Russian criminals ran a trafficking ring in 1991 in Canada involving eleven women from the Newly Independent States. The women came to work as models but were compelled to become strippers. They were forced to turn over their return airline tickets, passports, and cash for "safekeeping." Their handlers also reportedly kept them confined and forced them

---

[151] Global Survival Network, "Crime and Servitude: An Expose of the Traffic in Women for Prostitution from the Newly Independent States," October 1997.

[152] University of Pittsburgh, The Matthew B. Ridgway Center for International Security Studies, September 1999.

[153] Cable from the American Embassy in Tel Aviv, 008375, June 23, 1998.

[154] Vandenberg, Martina, Trafficking of Women to Israel and Forced Prostitution, A Report by the Israel Women's Network, November 1997.

[155] Cable from the American Embassy in Tel Aviv, 008375, June 23, 1998.

to turn over their earnings. They were made them to comply by threats of death and bodily harm to their loved ones in the Newly Independent States. Russian organized criminals have also been involved in extortion from women who have tried to come forward.[156]

Ukrainian Criminal Syndicates

Ukrainian organized crime groups are heavily involved in trafficking of women, according to the American Embassy in Kiev. Organized crime syndicates bribe Ukrainian immigration officials to look the other way, or in some cases, to facilitate the illegal entry or exit of undocumented or improperly documented women.[157] The International Organization for Migration reports that the majority of young Ukrainian women and girls are first recruited for ostensibly legal, mainly unskilled jobs before being forced into the sex business. The majority of the recruiters, who initiate the first contact with the victims, are young males between the ages of 20 and 25 years old. The recruiters are usually friends or acquaintances, or have made considerable efforts to gain their trust.[158]

Ukrainian crime groups reportedly control the prostitution markets in Hungary and Austria. A Ukrainian mafia boss was arrested in June 1997 at the Austrian/Italian border at Tarvisio. In cooperation with Albanian criminals, he had been trafficking dozens of Ukrainian girls to Italy and forcing them into prostitution.[159] The American Embassy in Ankara reports that

there are allegations that the Ukrainian mafia is turning women over to the Turkish mafia for $2,000 to $3,000 a woman.

Georgian Crime Groups

The American Embassy in T'bilisi reports that Georgian trafficking rings with strong ties to Russian organized crime traffic women through employment agencies used as fronts. Some rings specialize in trafficking women for the sex industry while others concentrate on labor exploitation. These organized rings traffic young women, between the ages of 16 and 30, to the United States for prostitution, while older women, 45 and above, may be trafficked for indentured servitude. The older women are aware they will be working as maids and nannies but unaware that they will be doing it for virtually no remuneration. The traffickers often supply the victims with counterfeit documents to obtain genuine visas and arrange for their travel to the US. Someone from the trafficking organization will meet them upon arrival at an US airport and confiscate their passports, stranding them in the US. Next, the women are placed in strip clubs, massage parlors, brothels, or households. They are expected to repay the traffickers for living expenses, transportation costs to the US, the costs of obtaining fraudulent documents, plus a penalizing interest on their debt. These women become in effect indentured servants, bound to work for free until their debts to the traffickers are repaid.[160]

Polish Crime Groups

In addition to being a source country, Poland is a transit country for women trafficked from other countries, such as Bulgaria, Romania and the Newly Independent States. The American Embassy in Warsaw reports that

---

[156] Cable from the American Embassy in Toronto, 001349, June 30, 1998.
[157] "Sources of Trafficked Women, Country Survey," Fraud Digest, Bureau of Consular Affairs, August 1998.
[158] International Organization for Migration, Information Campaign Against Trafficking in Women From Ukraine, Project Report, 1998.
[159] "Ukrainian Mafia Boss Arrested At Austrian Border," Rome Rai Uno Television Network, June 19, 1997.

---

[160] Cable from the American Embassy in T'bilisi, 03462, May 29, 1998.

Polish criminal networks recruit, transport, and deliver women from these countries into the hands of organized prostitution rings in destination countries. They may sell these women for about $30,000 each to Vietnamese, Ukrainian, Armenian, and Turkish gangs that dominate prostitution markets in Germany and other Western European countries. The new owners confiscate the women's travel documents and use beatings, gang rapes, and drugs to force them into prostitution. The women become virtual prisoners in the brothels, and are required to serve 10 to 20 clients a day.[161] There is also a growing tendency for victims to be drugged and kidnapped from public places, such as discos or pubs.[162] In Spain, Polish and Czech organized crime groups operate under the guise of travel agencies, according to the American Embassy in Madrid. They recruit the women and deliver them to their new handlers in Spain but are not involved in local prostitution. They use the threat of arrest and deportation to control the women.

Trafficking is also an efficiently cruel enterprise in Poland, which is increasingly becoming a destination country. Once the women and girls are brought to Poland, traffickers take away their passports and force them into prostitution to work off their debts and earn back their travel documents. Girls who resist are raped, beaten, or confined with minimal food and water until they comply. In some cases, girls have been killed for resisting trafficker's demands. Traffickers sink profits from their prostitution rings into illegal narcotics, weapons, or stolen cars.[163]

Many trafficking and prostitution enterprises are conducted by small organized rings of five to six persons, with criminal contacts. In some cases, these small rings are operated on the side by bigger trafficking rings. Generally, traffickers in both the origin and destination country have links to professional criminal organizations, which provide protection for the trafficker and brothels, and are used to intimidate the women. Many of the recruiters, who form the first contact with the victims, are young males between 20 and 25 years old, while the trafficker who runs the operation is generally between 20 and 55 years old.[164]

Albanian Crime Groups

Albanian criminal groups are rapidly expanding their organized drug networks to include prostitution rings that operate in northern Italy. The Executive Director of UNICEF, Carol Bellamy, says there is growing evidence of trafficking in girls from Albania to Italy.[165] Criminal clans, often based on family ties, target orphans and young girls from large families in Albania and lure them abroad with promises of marriage and/or jobs as waitresses or domestics. The American Consulate in Milan reports that a recent development is the increase in trafficking of minors, primarily Albanians, spawned by the hope that young girls are free of AIDs. Typically, the criminals smuggle the girls by rubber dinghy from Valona in southern Albania to Puglia in southern Italy. From there, they transport them to northern Italy via taxi, train, or semi-trucks.[166]

Albanian criminals are also taking advantage of broken-up families and confusion in the refugee camps in neighboring countries to target and traffic Kosovo minors for adoption or the sex industry.[167] Girls have ended up in

[161] "Sources of Trafficked Women: Country Survey," Fraud Digest, Bureau of Consular Affairs, August 1998.
[162] Cable from the American Embassy in Warsaw, Poland, 002745, March 19, 1999.
[163] Cable from the American Embassy in Warsaw, Poland, 002745, March 19, 1999.

[164] Report of the Mission of the Special Rapporteur on violence against women and her mission to Poland on the issue of trafficking and forced prostitution, June 1997.
[165] "UNICEF Sees Prostitution Among Kosovo Albanians," Reuters, May 20, 1999.
[166] Cable from American Consulate Milan 000757, September 11, 1998.

prostitution and child exploitation rings in northern Italy, especially Turin and Milan. The American Consulate in Milan also reports that there is growing evidence of torture and terror by the Albanian criminals in order to keep these girls in line. Uncooperative girls have been killed. Dr. Pier Luigi Vigna, Italy's National Anti-Mafia Prosecutor, concurs about the extreme violence of the Albanian crime groups, noting a case where Albanian girls were tattooed with the crime group's symbols. In other cases, the Albanians have burned their victims for punishment.[168]

General Francesco Saverio Polella, head of the National Investigation Division of Italy's Anti-Mafia Directorate, said in July that Albanian and Italian crime groups are cooperating in transporting drugs and trafficking women and girls into Italy. Once in Italy, the Albanians are managing the selling of the women and girls into prostitution. One Albanian women's organization concluded in a study that Albanian gangs sell the girls to criminal organizations in Italy and/or Greece for $10,000. To facilitate their business and these transactions, Mr. Polella also claims that the Albanian crime groups have divided up specific tasks, such as recruitment, transportation, and prostitution, amongst themselves in their trafficking operations.

Some experts claim that Albanian criminal organizations are also recruiting directly in Belgian refugee centers. Albanian criminal groups are taking control of prostitution networks in Belgium, particularly Antwerp and Brussels. These gangs have now established territorial control of the streets and districts where they are free to develop other criminal activities, such as drug trafficking and racketeering. Girls brought to Belgium by other criminal organizations are being "stolen" from

them by the Albanians. By some accounts, the Albanians are believed to be working as subcontractors for the Turkish mafia, whose members are increasingly distancing themselves from the operational level, for heroin trafficking. The traditional intermediaries, previously French, Moroccans and Turks, have been supplanted by Albanians, either from Albania or Kosovo.[169]

Nigerian Crime Rings

The American Embassy in Lagos reports that trafficking in women tends to be more of a localized cottage industry than an organized racket involving Nigerian criminal syndicates.[170] Italian prosecutors believe that Nigerian rings are trafficking women to and within Italy for the sex industry. The American Consulate in Milan reports that a Nigerian slave trade operates in Genoa, Italy. Nigerian women and men have been involved in abetting illegal immigration, reducing girls to slavery, forcing them into prostitution, and exploiting them for profit. Girls from Africa are lured to Italy with promises of work as bar girls, waitresses, or models. They are then forced upon arrival to undress and promenade nude before fellow Nigerians who pay $9,000 to $30,000 depending on the girls' age and physical attributes. The women and girls are kept in submission by threats, voodoo, and magic.[171] In Naples, Italy's National Anti-Mafia Prosecutor said in July that the Camorra, an Italian organized crime group, rent streets to Nigerians whom have trafficked Nigerian women to Italy for prostitution. In Spain, the American Embassy in Madrid reports that the African trafficking rings are the least organized and sophisticated of the trafficking organizations operating there. They rely on force to maintain discipline.

---

[167] "UNHCR Chief Says Refugees Forced Into Prostitution," Reuters, May 5, 1999 and cable from the American Embassy in Rome 02493, April 19, 1999.
[168] Discussions with the US-Italy Bilateral Working Group on Trafficking in Women, July 1999.

[169] FBIS, April 15, 1998.
[170] Cable from the American Embassy in Lagos, 007146, July 16, 1999.
[171] Cable from the American Consulate in Milan, 000942, November 10, 1998.

Bibliography

Cases (Indictments, Affidavits)

- US v. Bonds, Indictment, CR 93, US District Court for the Eastern District of North Carolina, Raleigh Division.

- US v. Cadena, Superseding Indictment, Case No. 98-14015-CR-RYSKAMP, US District Court, Southern District of Florida, April 23, 1998; Videotaped deposition of a victim, November 5, 1998; Victim Impact Letters.

- US v. Cam, US District Court for the Central District of California, CR 96-459, June 1995.

- US v. Cortez, Indictment, 2:97-560, US District Court of South Carolina, Charleston Division, June 18, 1997.

- US v. Driggers, 2:97, US District Court of South Carolina, Charleston Division, May 8, 1997.

- US v. Flores, Indictment, 2:96-806, US District Court of South Carolina, Charleston Division, October 10, 1996.

- US v. Kwon, Indictment, US District Court for the Northern Mariana Islands, CR 98-00044, November 1998.

- US v. Lozano, Indictment, EP 98 CR 0335, US District Court for the Western District of Texas, El Paso Division, March 1998.

- US v. Manasurangkun, Superseding Indictment, CR 95-714 (A), US District Court for the Central District of California, February 1995; Government's Filing of the Original Executed Plea Agreement, CR 95-714 (B), US District Court for the Central District of California, February 9, 1996.

- US v. Mishulovich, Superseding Indictment, US District Court, Northern District of Illinois, Eastern Division, April 22, 1999; FBI Affidavit, September 9, 1998.

- US v. Paoletti, Indictment, CR 97 768, US District Court Eastern District of New York, August 19, 1998; Superseding Information.

- US v. Ruc, Diplomatic Security, Criminal Intelligence Report, V-96-00098, March 1998.

- US v. Wattanasiri, Indictment, S.R. 95 Cr. 52, US District Court, Southern District of New York.

- US v. Wuttidetgrienggrai, Indictment, 95 Cr. 200, US District Court, Southern District of New York.

- Class Action, AFL-CIO, Global Exchange, Sweatshop Watch, Union of Needletrades Industrial and Textile Employees, and Asian Law Caucus. v. The Gap, The Associated Merchandising Corp., Cutter and Buck, Inc., Dayton-Hudson Corp., The Dress Barn, The Gymboree Corp., J.C. Penney Company, J.Crew Group, Jones Apparel Group, Lady Bryant, The Limited, The May Department, Nordstrom, Oshkosh B'Gosh, Sears Roebuck and Company, Tommy Hilfiger, Wal-Mart, Warnaco Group, and Does 1-400, US District Court for the Central District of California, 1999.

Dailies, Quarterlies

- Department of Justice, Immigration and Naturalization Service, "Borderline," Intelligence Daily Report, September 1998 – October 1999.

- Department of State, Bureau of Consular Affairs Fraud Prevention Programs, Monthly Bulletins.

- Gender Matters Quarterly, USAID Office of Women in Development, Gender Research Project, "Women as Chattel: The Emerging Global Market in Trafficking," February 1999.

- International Organization for Migration, Trafficking in Migrants, Quarterly Bulletins, September 1998-September 1999.

Interviews

(T) indicates the interview was a telephone interview. Otherwise, the interview occurred in person.

Department of Justice
- Attorney General Janet Reno, September 1999.

- Public Policy Office, November 1998.

- Civil Rights Division, Criminal Section, October 1998, April, November 1999.

- Child Exploitation Obscenity Section, September 1998, August 1999.

- Office of International Affairs, November 1998.

- Office for Victims of Crimes, January 1999.

- Civil Rights Division, Office of Special Counsel for Immigration Related Unfair Employment Practices, March 1999.

- National Central Bureau for Interpol, March 1999 (T).

- DOJ worker abuse and exploitation one-day training course, Washington, DC, October 1998.

- Assistant US Attorney, Brooklyn, New York, December 1998.

- Assistant US Attorney, Los Angeles, California, February 1998.

- Assistant US Attorney, Miami, Florida, April 1999.

- Assistant US Attorney, Fort Lauderdale, Florida, May 1999 (T).

- Assistant US Attorney, New York, New York, May 1999.

- Assistant US Attorney, Chicago, Illinois, July 1999.

- Legal Attachés, Asia, Bangkok, Thailand, February 1999.

- Legal Attachés, Manila, Philippines, February 1999.

- International Law Enforcement Academy – Asia Director, Bangkok, Thailand, February 1999.

Federal Bureau of Investigation
- Intelligence Research Office, September, October 1998.

- FBI Agents, New York, December 1998.

- FBI Agent, West Palm Beach, April 1999.

- FBI Agent, Miami, August 1999 (T).

- FBI Headquarters, October 1999.

Immigration and Naturalization Service
- INS regional intelligence conference, New Orleans, Louisiana, September, 1999.

- INS Intelligence Workshop at the Naval Academy, Annapolis, Maryland, March 1999.

- INS Agent, Vancouver, Canada, August 1998.

- INS, Smuggling Criminal Organizations Branch, October 1998.

- INS Investigations, October 1998.

- INS Investigations, Field Operations, July 1999 (T).

- INS Agent, Louisville, Kentucky, October 1998 (T).

- INS Agent, New Orleans, November 1998 (T).

- INS Office of Detention and Deportation, November 1998.

- INS Agents, New York City, December 1998.

- INS Agents, Los Angeles, January 1999, September 1999 (T).

- INS Bangkok, Thailand February 1999.

- INS Manila, Philippines, February, 1999.

- INS Agent, Los Angeles, February 1999.

- INS, US Border Patrol, Anti-Smuggling Unit, April 1999.

- INS Agent, New York, May 1999.

- INS Juvenile Coordinator, August 1999 (T).

US Marshal Service
- US Marshal Service, Miami, Florida, May 1999 (T).

Drug Enforcement Agency
- DEA country attaché, Manila, Philippines, February 1999.

Department of Labor
- Wage and Hour Division, November 1999.

Department of State
- Deputy Chief of Mission, Bangkok, Thailand, February, 1999.

- Deputy Chief of Mission, Manila, Philippines, February 1999.

- President's Interagency Council on Women (constant and ongoing contact), September 1998 – October 1999.

- Bureau of International Narcotics and Law Enforcement Affairs (constant and ongoing contact), September 1998 – October 1999.

Bureau of Consular Affairs
- Office of Fraud Prevention Program, November, December 1998.

- Office of Visas, July 1999 (T).

- Consular Affairs, Vancouver, August 1999.

- Consular Affairs, Bangkok, Thailand, February 1999.

- Consular Affairs, Manila, Philippines, February 1999.

Diplomatic Security
- DS Agents, September, December, 1998, July 1999.

- DS Agent, Miami, Florida, April 1999 (T).

Agency for International Development
- USAID, Counselor, Manila, Philippines, February 1999.

- AID anti-trafficking team for Asia, March 1999.

Department of Treasury
- Customs officers, December 1998, January 1997.

State Police

- Washington, DC Police Academy, one-day training course on the sex industry in the US and child exploitation issues, November 1998.

- Maryland State Trooper, March 1999.

- New Jersey Law Enforcement, May 1999 (T).

- Florida Law Enforcement, Panama City, May 1999 (T).

Intelligence Community

- CIA Office of Transnational Issues, Crime and Narcotics Center.

- NSA.

Non-governmental Organizations

- Amnesty International officers, May 1999.

- Asian Women Human Rights Council, Quezon City, Philippines, February 1999.

- Batis Center for Women, Manila, Philippines, February 1999.

- Center for the Pacific-Asian Family, Outreach to Trafficking Victims, Los Angeles, California, February 1999.

- Coalition Against Trafficking Worldwide, New York, December 1998 Manila, Philippines, February 1999.

- End Child Prostitution, Child Pornography, and Trafficking in Children, Washington, DC, November 1999 Manila, Philippines, February 1999.

- Florida Immigrant Advocacy Center, West Palm Beach, Florida, April 1999.

- Global Survival Network, October 1998, April 1999, October 1999.

- Helping Individual Prostitutes Survive, October 1998 (T).

- Human Rights Watch, November 1998.

- India-Canada Cooperation Center, New Delhi, January 1999.

- International Human Rights Law Group, October 1998, November 1999.

- International Labor Organization, International Program on the Elimination of Child Labor, Bangkok, Thailand, February 1999.

- International Labor Rights Fund, October 1998.

- International Organization for Migration (IOM), Washington, DC, October, 1998.

- IOM, Bangkok, Thailand, February 1999.

- IOM, Manila, Philippines, February 1999.

- Legal Aid for Cambodia, November 1998.

- Little Tokyo Service Center, Coalition to Abolish Slavery and Trafficking, Los Angeles, California, February 1999.

- MiraMed Institute, November 1998, September 1999.

- National Center for Missing and Exploited Children, October 1998.

- OSCE, Office for Democratic Institutions and Human Rights, Poland, May 1999.

- Philippines American Services Group, November 1998.

- Philippine Network Against Trafficking of Women, Quezon City, Philippines, February 1999.

- Visayan Foundation, Manila, Philippines, February 1999.

- Women, Law, and Development, December 1998.

Academia
- Dr. Louise Shelley, American University, Director, Transnational Crime and Corruption Center, and Dr. Sally Stoecker, Human Trafficking Director and Research Professor, American University, Transnational Crime and Corruption Center, May 1999.

- Dr. Laura Lederer, Harvard University, The Protection Project, November 1998, July 1999.

- Dr. Kathryn McMahon, California State University, Associate Director Southeast Asian Studies Center, Professor International Studies and Women's Studies, February 1999 (T).

- Dr. Katharine Moon, Professor, Department of Political Science, Wellesley College, March 1999.

Foreign Government Officials
- Vilija Aleknaite-Abramikiene, Lithuanian Member of Parliament, October 9, 1999.

- Roundtable discussion in Vancouver, Canada on trafficking in women and children with representatives from the RCMP Criminal Investigations Unit, RCMP Immigration and Passport Section, RCMP General Investigation Section, British Columbia Ministry of the Attorney General, Canadian Citizenship and Immigration agency, August 1998.

- Met with South Asian (Bangladesh, India, Nepal, and Pakistan) trafficking experts, Washington, DC, September 1998.

- Roundtable discussion with trafficking in women experts from Russia, March 1999.

- Roundtable discussion with the Philippines Overseas Employment Administration, Filipino National Police Criminal Investigation Group, Philippine Anti-Organized Crime Task Force, Philippine Task Force on Illegal Recruitment, Manila, Philippines, February 1999.

- Philippines Department of Foreign Affairs, Office of European Affairs, and ASEAN office, Manila, Philippines, February 1999.

- Philippines Department of Justice, Bureau of Immigration, and Intelligence Division, Manila, Philippines, February 1999.

- Commission on Filipinos Overseas, Manila, Philippines, February 1999.

- The Netherlands, National Criminal Intelligence Division, Alien Smuggling Unit, Washington, DC, April 1999.

- Roundtable discussion, US/Italian Bilateral Working Group on Trafficking in Women, July 14-16, 1999.

Press
- Agence France Presse, "Japan Reports Rise in Foreigners Forced Into Prostitution," April 6, 1998.

- Agence France Presse, "Australia to Crack Down on Asian Sex Slaves," April 14, 1998.

- Associated Press, "Indictment Charges 23 Hmongs with Series of Rapes," October 20, 1999.

- Associated Press, "Police Bust California Sex-Slave Ring," November 19, 1998.

- Associated Press, "Police Break Up Sex-Slave Ring That Preyed On Immigrant Girls," November 13, 1998.

- Associated Press, "Two Plead Guilty in Mexican Baby Smuggling Case," July 15, 1999.

- Associated Press, "Adoptions of Smuggled Mexican Babies," July 25, 1999.

- Associated Press, "Prostitution Lord Admits Smuggling Mexican Women in the US as Sex Slaves," January 19, 1999.

- Associated Press, "Sisters Sentenced to Eight Years in Prison in Slave Labor Case," January 16, 1999.

- Barry, John, Miami Herald, "Tortured Au Pair Finds A New Life," July 31, 1998.

- Bennetto, Jason, "Triads Target British Sex Trade," The Independent, August 11, 1997.

- Booth, William, The Washington Post, "13 Charged in Gang Importing Prostitutes," August 21, 1999.

- Branigin, William, The Washington Post, "Modern-Day Slavery? Imported Servants Allege Abuse By Foreign Host Families in US," January 5, 1999.

- Branigin, William, The Washington Post, "A Life of Exhaustion, Beatings and Isolation," January 1999.

- Branigin, William, The Washington Post, "Human Rights Group Urges Action on Saipan," May 4, 1999.

- Daily Report China, "China: How Criminal Organizations Acquire Illicit Wealth," August 12, 1997.

- Johnston, Philip, "Triads and Mafia Cash In On Illegal Immigrants," The Daily Telegraph, November 27, 1997.

- Kleinfield, N.R., The New York Times, "Five Charged With Holding Thai Women Captive for Prostitution," December 20, 1995

- Korecki, Natasha, Chicago Daily Herald, "FBI Breaks Crime Rink Linked to Russian Mafia," September 19, 1998.

- Lardner, George, The Washington Post, "16 Charged With Forcing Mexicans Into Prostitution," April 24, 1998.

- Mercyhurst, "UN Representative to Travel to Guatemala to Assess Sale of Children," July 13, 1999.

- Miami Herald, "Haitian Girl Illegally Residing in the US, Sexually Abused and Forced to be a Maid," September 30, 1999.

- Navarro, Mireya, The New York Times, "Case of Florida Au Pair Reflects Wider Problem," December 12, 1998.

- Nicholson, Kieran and Wheeler, Sheba, Denver Post, "Three Held in Alleged Sex Slave Ring," November 13, 1998.

- Reuters, "Illegal Alien Heads Miami Forced Prostitution Ring," January 15, 1999.

- Reuters, "UNHCR Chief Says Refugees Forced Into Prostitution," May 5, 1999.

- Reuters, "UNICEF Sees Prostitution Among Kosovo Albanians," May 20, 1999.

- Shroder, Lisa, Sun-Sentinel, "The Servant's Tale," November 12, 1998.

- Smith, Stephanie, Palm Beach Daily, "Women Smuggled into US, Forced into Prostitution Try to Recoup $1 Million," April 8, 1999.

- "Not in This Country, They Can't," Editorial, The Washington Post, January, 7, 1999.

Reports and Papers

- Ad Hoc Committee on the Elaboration of a Convention against Transnational Organized Crime, revised draft Protocol to Prevent, Suppress and Punish Trafficking in Persons, especially Women and Children, Supplementing the United Nations Convention against Transnational Organized Crime, Fourth Session, Vienna, June 28 – July 9, 1999.

- Coalition Against Trafficking in Women, Trafficking in Women and Prostitution in the Asia Pacific, 1996.

- Congressman George Miller and the Democratic Staff of the House Committee on Resources, "Beneath the American Flag: Labor and Human Rights Abuses in CNMI," March 26, 1998.

- Foundation Against Trafficking in Women, International Human Rights Law Group, Global Alliance Against Traffic in Women, "Human Rights Standards for the Treatment of Trafficked Persons," 1999.

- Federal Bureau of Investigation, Asian Criminal Enterprise Unit, Trafficking of Asian Aliens, July 1998

- Global Survival Network, "Trapped: Human Trafficking for Forced Labor in The Commonwealth of the Northern Mariana Islands, a US Territory," 1999.

- Global Survival Network, "Crime and Servitude: An Exposé of the Traffic in Women for Prostitution from the Newly Independent States," October 1997.

- Hughes, Donna, and Roche, Claire, Making the Harm Visible, Global Sexual Exploitation of Women and Girls, Coalition Against Trafficking in Women, Kingston, Rhode Island, February 1999.

- Hughes, Donna, The Coalition Against Trafficking in Women, "Pimps and Predators on the Internet, Globalizing the Sexual Exploitation of Women and Children," Rhode Island, March 1999.

- Human Rights Watch, United States, "Locked Away: Immigration Detainees in Jails in the United States," Vol. 10, No. 1, September 1998.

- Immigration and Naturalization Service, Backgrounder on Trafficking Enforcement Case Summaries, October 23, 1998.

- Immigration and Naturalization Service, Operation Lost Thai Special Report, September 28, 1999.

- International Criminal Police Organization, (Interpol), Bird, Yoshi, "The Challenges Posed by Insufficient Collaboration and Communication in the Pro-Active Fight against Trafficking in Women, A Victim-Centered Approach to Anti-Trafficking Work," Lyon, France, September 1999.

- Interpol, Bird, Yoshi, Draft copy, "The Trafficking of Children for Sexual Exploitation and Foreign Adoption: Background and Current Measures," Lyon, France, September 1999.

- Interpol, International Conference on Trafficking in Women, Vienna, Austria 20 – October 21, 1998.

- International Center for Migration Policy Development, "Draft Study on the Relationship Between Organised Crime and Trafficking in Aliens," Prepared by the Secretariat of the Budapest Group, Vienna, Austria, January 1999.

- International Organization for Migration, "Feasibility Study on Rapid Information Transfer Aiming at Preventing and Combating Trafficking in Human Beings, in Particular Women and Children, for Sexual Exploitation in the European Union," European Commission, Task Force Justice and Home Affairs, STOP-Programme 1998/99.

- International Organization for Migration, "Information Campaign Against Trafficking in Women From Ukraine," Project Report, July 1998.

- International Organization for Migration, Subregional Office for East Asia and Oceania, Support to Trafficked and Other Vulnerable Women Migrant Workers in the Commonwealth of Northern Mariana Islands.

- Israel Women's Network, Trafficking of Women to Israel and Forced Prostitution, November 1997.

- Lederer, Laura, Dr., The Protection Project, "The Sex Trade: Trafficking of Women and Children in Europe and the United States, report for the Commission on Security and Cooperation in Europe," June 1999.

- Lederer, Laura, Dr., The Protection Project— Creating an International Framework for Legislation to Protect Women and Children from Commercial Sexual Exploitation.

- Information on the legislation, information on national and international legislation protecting women and children from commercial sexual exploitation.

- Miller, Ali and Stewart, Alison, International Human Rights Law Group, "Report from the Roundtable on The Meaning of Trafficking in Persons: A Human Rights Perspective," Women's Rights Law Reporter, Rutgers Law School, Fall/Winter 1998, Volume 20, Number 1.

- Pilkerton, Chris, "Traffic Jam: Recommendations for Civil and Criminal Penalties to Curb the Recent Trafficking of Women from Post-Cold War Russia," Michigan Journal of Gender and Law, 1999.

- Report of the Mission of the Special Rapporteur on Violence Against Women and Her Mission to Poland on the Issue of Trafficking and Forced Prostitution, May 24 – June 1997.

- Skrobanek, Siriporn, Boonpakdi, Nattaya, Janthakeero, Chutima, The Traffic in Women, Human Realities of the International Sex Trade, Zed Book Ltd., London and New York, 1997.

- The Hague, Ministerial Declaration on European Guidelines for Effective Measures to Prevent and Combat Trafficking in Women for the Purpose of Sexual Exploitation, Ministerial Conference, The Hague, April 24-26, 1997.

- Trends in Organized Crime, Special Focus: Modern Slavery: Trafficking in Women and Children, Transnational Periodicals Consortium with the National Strategy Information Center, Summer 1998, Volume 3, Number 4.

- UNIFEM, Trade in Human Misery, Trafficking in Women and Children, Asia Region, November 1998

- United Nations, Report of the Secretary General, "Traffic in Women and Girls," September 1997.

- UN Crime Commission: Report on the 6th Session of the UN Commission on Crime Prevention and Criminal Justice, April 1997.

State Department Cables

US embassies around the world have reported on trafficking in women and children. Trafficking reports have been sent in from embassies in the following countries:

- Austria, Australia, Bangladesh, Belarus, Belgium, Brazil, Bulgaria, Burma, Canada, Czech Republic, Dominican Republic, Georgia, Greece, India, Indonesia, Ireland, Israel, Italy, Japan, Laos, Lithuania, Luxembourg, Malaysia, Moldova, Nepal, Nigeria, Pakistan, the Philippines, Poland, Romania, Russia, Singapore, Spain, South Korea, Sweden, Taiwan, Thailand, The Netherlands, The Vatican, Turkey, Turkmenistan, UAE, Ukraine, United Kingdom, and Vietnam.

Videos, Films, and Documentaries

- Bruno, Ellen, "Sacrifice," (Trafficking in Women and Girls in Southeast Asia), 1998.

- Department of Justice, Office for Victims of Crime, "A Balance to Maintain," INS Informational Training Video.

- Global Survival Network, "Bought and Sold," (An Exposé of the Traffic in Women for Prostitution from the Newly Independent States), 1998.

- Gupta, Ruchira, "The Selling of Innocents," (Trafficking in Women and Girls in South Asia), December 1996.

- Soki Paulin Ballesteros, International Organization for Migration, "Sex Trafficking: We're So Syndicated, Ma'am," public education video in the Philippines.

- Transnational Seminar on Trafficking in Women, Budapest, June 1998.

Others

- Attended the Global Conference on Trafficking and Sexual Exploitation, January 26-29, 1999, Dhaka, Bangladesh.

- Debrief of a trafficking victim from the Czech Republic, New York, December 1998.

- Debrief of a trafficker, West Palm Beach, Florida, April 1999.